MznLnx

Missing Links Exam Preps

Exam Prep for

Intermediate Accounting: Volume 1

Kieso, Weygandt, Warfield, 12th Edition

The MznLnx Exam Prep is your link from the texbook and lecture to your exams.
The MznLnx Exam Preps are unauthorized and comprehensive reviews of your textbooks.

All material provided by MznLnx and Rico Publications (c) 2010
Textbook publishers and textbook authors do not particpate in or contribute to these reviews.

MznLnx

Rico
Publications

Exam Prep for Intermediate Accounting: Volume 1
12th Edition
Kieso, Weygandt, Warfield

Publisher: Raymond Houge
Assistant Editor: Michael Rouger
Text and Cover Designer: Lisa Buckner
Marketing Manager: Sara Swagger
Project Manager, Editorial Production: Jerry Emerson
Art Director: Vernon Lowerui

Product Manager: Dave Mason
Editorial Assitant: Rachel Guzmanji
Pedagogy: Debra Long
Cover Image: Jim Reed/Getty Images
Text and Cover Printer: City Printing, Inc.
Compositor: Media Mix, Inc.

(c) 2010 Rico Publications
ALL RIGHTS RESERVED. No part of this work covered by the copyright may be reproduced or used in any form or by an means--graphic, electronic, or mechanical, including photocopying, recording, taping, Web distribution, information storage, and retrieval systems, or in any other manner--without the written permission of the publisher.

Printed in the United States
ISBN:

For more information about our products, contact us at:
Dave.Mason@RicoPublications.com

For permission to use material from this text or product, submit a request online to:
Dave.Mason@RicoPublications.com

Contents

CHAPTER 1
Financial Accounting and Accounting Standards,   1

CHAPTER 2
Conceptual Framework Underlying Financial Accounting,   11

CHAPTER 3
The Accounting Information System,   13

CHAPTER 4
Income Statement and Related Information,   26

CHAPTER 5
Balance Sheet and Statement of Cash Flows,   32

CHAPTER 6
Accounting and the Time Value of Money,   43

CHAPTER 7
Cash and Receivables,   53

CHAPTER 8
Valuation of Inventories: A Cost-Basis Approach,   68

CHAPTER 9
Inventories: Additional Valuation Issues,   76

CHAPTER 10
Acquisition and Disposition of Property, Plant, and Equipment,   84

CHAPTER 11
Depreciation, Impairments, and Depletion,   90

CHAPTER 12
Intangible Assets,   100

CHAPTER 13
Current Liabilities and Contingencies,   104

CHAPTER 14
Long-Term Liabilities,   117

ANSWER KEY   132

TO THE STUDENT

COMPREHENSIVE

The *MznLnx* Exam Prep series is designed to help you pass your exams. Editors at MznLnx review your textbooks and then prepare these practice exams to help you master the textbook material. Unlike study guides, workbooks, and practice tests provided by the texbook publisher and textbook authors, *MznLnx* gives you **all** of the material in each chapter in exam form, not just samples, so you can be sure to nail your exam.

MECHANICAL

The MznLnx Exam Prep series creates exams that will help you learn the subject matter as well as test you on your understanding. Each question is designed to help you master the concept. Just working through the exams, you gain an understanding of the subject--its a simple mechanical process that produces success.

INTEGRATED STUDY GUIDE AND REVIEW

MznLnx is not just a set of exams designed to test you, its also a comprehensive review of the subject content. Each exam question is also a review of the concept, making sure that you will get the answer correct without having to go to other sources of material. You learn as you go! Its the easiest way to pass an exam.

HUMOR

Studying can be tedious and dry. MznLnx's instructional design includes moderate humor within the exam questions on occassion, to break the tedium and revitalize the brain

Chapter 1. Financial Accounting and Accounting Standards, 1

1. _____ measures the nominal future sum of money that a given sum of money is 'worth' at a specified time in the future assuming a certain interest rate rate of return; it is the present value multiplied by the accumulation function.

The value does not include corrections for inflation or other factors that affect the true value of money in the future. This is used in time value of money calculations.

   a. Present value
   c. Net present value
   b. 3M Company
   d. Future value

2. _____ is the value on a given date of a future payment or series of future payments, discounted to reflect the time value of money and other factors such as investment risk. _____ calculations are widely used in business and economics to provide a means to compare cash flows at different times on a meaningful 'like to like' basis.

The most commonly applied model of the time value of money is compound interest.

   a. Net present value
   c. 3M Company
   b. Future value
   d. Present value

3. The term _____ is used in finance theory to refer to any terminating stream of fixed payments over a specified period of time. This usage is most commonly seen in academic discussions of finance, usually in connection with the valuation of the stream of payments, taking into account time value of money concepts such as interest rate and future value.

Examples of these are regular deposits to a savings account, monthly home mortgage payments and monthly insurance payments.

   a. Improvement
   c. Intangible
   b. Appropriation
   d. Annuity

4. _____ is concerned with the provisions and use of accounting information to managers within organizations, to provide them with the basis to make informed business decisions that will allow them to be better equipped in their management and control functions.

In contrast to financial accountancy information, _____ information is:

- usually confidential and used by management, instead of publicly reported;
- forward-looking, instead of historical;
- pragmatically computed using extensive management information systems and internal controls, instead of complying with accounting standards.

This is because of the different emphasis: _____ information is used within an organization, typically for decision-making.

   a. Grenzplankostenrechnung
   c. Governmental accounting
   b. Management accounting
   d. Nonassurance services

Chapter 1. Financial Accounting and Accounting Standards,

5. In economics, _____ or _____ goods or real _____ refers to factors of production used to create goods or services that are not themselves significantly consumed (though they may depreciate) in the production process. _____ goods may be acquired with money or financial _____. In finance and accounting, _____ generally refers to financial wealth, especially that used to start or maintain a business.

   a. Disclosure
   b. Vyborg Appeal
   c. Screening
   d. Capital

6. The _____ founded on April 1, 2001 is the successor of the International Accounting Standards Committee (IASC) founded in June 1973 in London. It is responsible for developing the International Financial Reporting Standards (new name for the International Accounting Standards issued after 2001), and promoting the use and application of these standards.

   The _____ is an independent, privately-funded accounting standard-setter based in London, UK.

   a. Information Systems Audit and Control Association
   b. Emerging technologies
   c. Institute of Management Accountants
   d. International Accounting Standards Board

7. An _____ is a comprehensive report on a company's activities throughout the preceding year. _____s are intended to give shareholders and other interested persons information about the company's activities and financial performance. Most jurisdictions require companies to prepare and disclose _____s, and many require the _____ to be filed at the company's registry.

   a. ABC Television Network
   b. Annual report
   c. AMEX
   d. AIG

8. The _____ is a private, not-for-profit organization whose primary purpose is to develop generally accepted accounting principles (GAAP) within the United States in the public's interest. The Securities and Exchange Commission (SEC) designated the _____ as the organization responsible for setting accounting standards for public companies in the U.S. It was created in 1973, replacing the Accounting Principles Board and the Committee on Accounting Procedure of the American Institute of Certified Public Accountants. The _____'s mission is 'to establish and improve standards of financial accounting and reporting for the guidance and education of the public, including issuers, auditors, and users of financial information.'

   The _____ is not a governmental body.

   a. Public company
   b. Governmental Accounting Standards Board
   c. Fannie Mae
   d. Financial Accounting Standards Board

9. _____ is an acronym for First In, First Out, an abstraction in ways of organizing and manipulation of data relative to time and prioritization. This expression describes the principle of a queue processing technique or servicing conflicting demands by ordering process by first-come, first-served (FCFS) behaviour: what comes in first is handled first, what comes in next waits until the first is finished, etc.

Thus it is analogous to the behaviour of persons queueing (or 'standing in line', in common American parlance), where the persons leave the queue in the order they arrive, or waiting one's turn at a traffic control signal.

Chapter 1. Financial Accounting and Accounting Standards,

a. FIFO
b. Risk management
c. Kanban
d. Trademark

10. In business and accounting, _____ are everything of value that is owned by a person or company. It is a claim on the property your income of a borrower. The balance sheet of a firm records the monetary value of the _____ owned by the firm.

a. Earnings before interest, taxes, depreciation and amortization
b. Accrual basis accounting
c. Accounts receivable
d. Assets

11. _____ is the difference between the cost of a good or service and its selling price. A _____ is added on to the total cost incurred by the producer of a good or service in order to create a profit. The total cost reflects the total amount of both fixed and variable expenses to produce and distribute a product.

a. Statements of Financial Accounting Standards No. 133, Accounting for Derivative Instruments and Hedging Activities
b. Merck ' Co., Inc.
c. Corporate Bond
d. Markup

12. _____ is the balance of the amounts of cash being received and paid by a business during a defined period of time, sometimes tied to a specific project. Measurement of _____ can be used

- to evaluate the state or performance of a business or project.
- to determine problems with liquidity. Being profitable does not necessarily mean being liquid. A company can fail because of a shortage of cash, even while profitable.
- to project rate of returns. The time of _____s into and out of projects are used as inputs to financial models such as internal rate of return, and net present value.
- to examine income or growth of a business when it is believed that accrual accounting concepts do not represent economic realities. Alternately, _____ can be used to 'validate' the net income generated by accrual accounting.

_____ as a generic term may be used differently depending on context, and certain _____ definitions may be adapted by analysts and users for their own uses. Common terms include operating _____ and free _____.

a. Controlling interest
b. Commercial paper
c. Flow-through entity
d. Cash flow

13. In economic models, the _____ time frame assumes no fixed factors of production. Firms can enter or leave the marketplace, and the cost (and availability) of land, labor, raw materials, and capital goods can be assumed to vary. In contrast, in the short-run time frame, certain factors are assumed to be fixed, because there is not sufficient time for them to change.

a. 3M Company
b. Long-run
c. Short-run
d. BMC Software, Inc.

14. _____ is that which is owed; usually referencing assets owed, but the term can also cover moral obligations and other interactions not requiring money. In the case of assets, _____ is a means of using future purchasing power in the present before a summation has been earned. Some companies and corporations use _____ as a part of their overall corporate finance strategy.

   a. Loan   b. Debenture
   c. Debt   d. Lender

15. _____ are formal records of a business' financial activities.

In British English, including United Kingdom company law, _____ are often referred to as accounts, although the term _____ is also used, particularly by accountants.

_____ provide an overview of a business' financial condition in both short and long term.

   a. 3M Company   b. Notes to the financial statements
   c. Statement of retained earnings   d. Financial statements

16. _____ were published by Accounting Principles Board (APB.) The board was created by American Institute of Certified Public Accountants (AICPA) in 1959 and was replaced by Financial Accounting Standards Board (FASB) in 1973. Its mission was to develop an overall conceptual framework of US generally accepted accounting principles (US GAAP.)

   a. Accounting Principles Board Opinions   b. ABC Television Network
   c. AIG   d. AMEX

17. An _____ is a practitioner of accountancy, which is the measurement, disclosure or provision of assurance about financial information that helps managers, investors, tax authorities and other decision makers make resource allocation decisions.

The word '_____' is derived from the French 'Compter' which took its origin from the Latin 'Computare'. The word was formerly written in English as 'Accomptant', but in process of time the word, which was always pronounced by dropping the 'p', became gradually changed both in pronunciation and in orthography to its present form.

   a. ABC Television Network   b. AIG
   c. AMEX   d. Accountant

18. The _____ is the national, professional association of CPAs in the United States, with more than 330,000 members, including CPAs in business and industry, public practice, government, and education; student affiliates; and international associates. It sets ethical standards for the profession and U.S. auditing standards for audits of private companies; federal, state and local governments; and non-profit organizations.

Approximately 40% of its members are engaged in the practice of public accounting, in areas such as auditing, accounting, taxation, general business consulting, business valuation, personal financial planning and business technology.

Chapter 1. Financial Accounting and Accounting Standards,

a. AIG
b. ABC Television Network
c. American Institute of Certified Public Accountants
d. Other postemployment benefits

19. _____ is the statutory title of qualified accountants in the United States who have passed the Uniform _____ Examination and have met additional state education and experience requirements for certification as a _____. Individuals who have passed the Exam but have not either accomplished the required on-the-job experience or have previously met it but in the meantime have lapsed their continuing professional education are, in many states, permitted the designation '_____ Inactive' or an equivalent phrase. In most U.S. states, only _____s who are licensed are able to provide to the public attestation (including auditing) opinions on financial statements.

a. Certified General Accountant
b. Chartered Accountant
c. Chartered Certified Accountant
d. Certified Public Accountant

20. _____ is the term used to refer to the standard framework of guidelines for financial accounting used in any given jurisdiction. _____ includes the standards, conventions, and rules accountants follow in recording and summarizing transactions, and in the preparation of financial statements.

Financial accounting information must be assembled and reported objectively.

a. Current asset
b. Generally accepted accounting principles
c. Long-term liabilities
d. General ledger

21. _____ is any physical or virtual entity that is owned by an individual or jointly by a group of individuals. An owner of _____ has the right to consume, sell, rent, mortgage, transfer and exchange his or her _____. Important widely-recognized types of _____ include real _____, personal _____ (other physical possessions), and intellectual _____ (rights over artistic creations, inventions, etc.), although the latter is not always as widely recognized or enforced.

a. Property
b. Fiduciary
c. Primary authority
d. Disclosure requirement

22. _____, also known as property, plant, and equipment (PP&E), is a term used in accountancy for assets and property which cannot easily be converted into cash. This can be compared with current assets such as cash or bank accounts, which are described as liquid assets. In most cases, only tangible assets are referred to as fixed.

a. Subledger
b. Minority interest
c. Bankruptcy prediction
d. Fixed asset

23. The U.S. _____ is an independent agency of the United States government which holds primary responsibility for enforcing the federal securities laws and regulating the securities industry, the nation's stock and options exchanges, and other electronic securities markets. The SEC was created by section 4 of the Securities Exchange Act of 1934 (now codified as 15 U.S.C. ÂÂ§ 78d and commonly referred to as the 1934 Act.)

a. Securities and Exchange Commission
b. BNSF Railway
c. 3M Company
d. BMC Software, Inc.

24. A _____ is a fungible, negotiable instrument representing financial value. they are broadly categorized into debt securities (such as banknotes, bonds and debentures), and equity securities; e.g., common stocks. The company or other entity issuing the _____ is called the issuer.

a. Security
b. BMC Software, Inc.
c. Tracking stock
d. 3M Company

25. The _____ is the former authoritative body of the American Institute of Certified Public Accountants (AICPA.) It was created by the American Institute of Certified Public Accountants in 1959 and issued pronouncements on accounting principles until 1973, when it was replaced by the Financial Accounting Standards Board (FASB.)

The _____ was disbanded in the hopes that the smaller, fully-independent FASB could more effectively create accounting standards.

a. American Payroll Association
b. Institute of Management Accountants
c. International Federation of Accountants
d. Accounting Principles Board

26. _____ were documents issued by the Committee on Accounting Procedure between 1938 and 1959 on various accounting problems. They were discontinued with the dissolution of the Committee in 1959 under a recommendation from the Special Committee on Research Program. In all, 51 bulletins were issued, however, the lack of binding authority over AICPA's membership reduced the influence of, and compliance with the content of the bulletins.

a. Other postemployment benefits
b. ABC Television Network
c. AIG
d. Accounting Research Bulletins

27. The _____ was a predecessor of the Accounting Principles Board, itself a predecessor to the Financial Accounting Standards Board in the United States. Its formation and activities were early efforts to rationalize and legitimize the reporting of business performance. However, it is widely regarded as having failed.

a. Price variance
b. Committee on Accounting Procedure
c. Lump sum
d. Consolidated financial statements

28. The _____ is located in Norwalk, Connecticut. It is an independent, organization in the private sector that is responsible for oversight of the Financial Accounting Standards Board (FASB), the Governmental Accounting Standards Board (GASB), and their respective advisory councils.

a. BMC Software, Inc.
b. BNSF Railway
c. Financial Accounting Foundation
d. 3M Company

29. _____ methods are means of managing inventory and financial matters involving the money a company ties up within inventory of produced goods, raw materials, parts, components, or feed stocks. FIFO stands for first-in, first-out, meaning that the oldest inventory items are recorded as sold first. LIFO stands for last-in, first-out, meaning that the most recently purchased items are recorded as sold first.

a. 3M Company
b. Finished good
c. Reorder point
d. FIFO and LIFO accounting

30. The _____ is currently the source of generally accepted accounting principles (GAAP) used by State and Local governments in the [[United States of America]]. As with most of the entities involved in creating GAAP in the United States, it is a private, non-governmental organization.

The _____ is subject to oversight by the Financial Accounting Foundation (FAF), which selects the members of the _____ and the Financial Accounting Standards Board, and funds both organizations.

a. Fannie Mae
b. National Conference of Commissioners on Uniform State Laws
c. Governmental Accounting Standards Board
d. Multinational corporation

31. _____ is an umbrella term which refers to the various accounting systems used by various public sector entities. In the United States, for instance, there are two levels of government which follow different accounting standards set forth by independent, private sector boards. At the federal level, the Federal Accounting Standards Advisory Board (FASAB) sets forth the accounting standards to follow.

a. Product control
b. Nonassurance services
c. Governmental Accounting
d. Management accounting

32. Book Value = Original Cost - _____

Book value at the end of year becomes book value at the beginning of next year. The asset is depreciated until the book value equals scrap value.

If the vehicle were to be sold and the sales price exceeded the depreciated value (net book value) then the excess would be considered a gain and subject to depreciation recapture.

a. AMEX
b. ABC Television Network
c. AIG
d. Accumulated Depreciation

33. _____ is a term used in accounting, economics and finance to spread the cost of an asset over the span of several years.

In simple words we can say that _____ is the reduction in the value of an asset due to usage, passage of time, wear and tear, technological outdating or obsolescence, depletion, inadequacy, rot, rust, decay or other such factors.

In accounting, _____ is a term used to describe any method of attributing the historical or purchase cost of an asset across its useful life, roughly corresponding to normal wear and tear.

a. General ledger
b. Net profit
c. Current asset
d. Depreciation

34. In the United States, the _____ is the senior technical committee designated by the American Institute of Certified Public Accountants (AICPA) to issue auditing, attestation, and quality control statements, standards and guidance to certified public accountants (CPAs) for non-public company audits. Created in October 1978, it is composed of 19 members representing various industries and sectors, including public accountants and private, educational, and governmental entities. It issues pronouncements in the form of statements, interpretations, and guidelines, which all CPAs must adhere to when performing audits and attestations.

a. Assurance service
b. Engagement Letter
c. Information audit
d. Auditing Standards Board

35. The _____ of 2002 (Pub.L. 107-204, 116 Stat. 745, enacted July 30, 2002), also known as the Public Company Accounting Reform and Investor Protection Act of 2002, is a United States federal law enacted on July 30, 2002 in response to a number of major corporate and accounting scandals including those affecting Enron, Tyco International, Adelphia, Peregrine Systems and WorldCom. The legislation establishes new or enhanced standards for all U.S. public company boards, management, and public accounting firms. It does not apply to privately held companies.
 a. Lease   b. Fair Labor Standards Act
 c. FCPA   d. Sarbanes-Oxley Act

36. In financial accounting, a _____ is defined as an obligation of an entity arising from past transactions or events, the settlement of which may result in the transfer or use of assets, provision of services or other yielding of economic benefits in the future.
 a. Vested   b. Liability
 c. False Claims Act   d. Corporate governance

37. An _____ is a term used in behavioral economics to describe those types of behaviors that impose costs on a person in the long-run that are not taken into account when making decisions in the present. Classical Economics discourages government from creating legislation that targets internalities, because it is assumed that the consumer takes these personal costs into account when paying for the good that causes the _____. For example, cigarettes should be taxed because of the negative consumption externalities that they impose, such as second-hand smoke, not because the smoker harms him or herself by smoking.
 a. Authorised capital   b. Inventory turnover ratio
 c. Internality   d. Operating budget

38. In accounting and organizational theory, _____ is defined as a process effected by an organization's structure, work and authority flows, people and management information systems, designed to help the organization accomplish specific goals or objectives. It is a means by which an organization's resources are directed, monitored, and measured. It plays an important role in preventing and detecting fraud and protecting the organization's resources, both physical (e.g., machinery and property) and intangible (e.g., reputation or intellectual property such as trademarks.)
 a. Internal control   b. Auditor independence
 c. Audit risk   d. Audit committee

39. The _____ (sometimes called 'Peekaboo') is a private-sector, non-profit corporation created by the Sarbanes-Oxley Act, a 2002 United States federal law, to oversee the auditors of public companies. Its stated purpose is to 'protect the interests of investors and further the public interest in the preparation of informative, fair, and independent audit reports'. Although a private entity, the _____ has many government-like regulatory functions, making it in some ways similar to the private Self Regulatory Organizations (SROs) that regulate stock markets and other aspects of the financial markets in the United States.
 a. 3M Company   b. Financial Crimes Enforcement Network
 c. Pension Benefit Guaranty Corporation   d. Public Company Accounting Oversight Board

40. The term _____ usually refers to a company that is permitted to offer its registered securities (stock, bonds, etc.) for sale to the general public, typically through a stock exchange, or occasionally a company whose stock is traded over the counter (OTC) via market makers who use non-exchange quotation services.

The term '_____' may also refer to a company owned by the government.

Chapter 1. Financial Accounting and Accounting Standards,

a. Governmental Accounting Standards Board
b. Professional association
c. MicroStrategy
d. Public Company

41. _____ is the corporate management term for the act of partially dismantling or otherwise reorganizing a company for the purpose of making it more profitable. Also known as corporate _____, debt _____ and financial _____.

_____ is often done as part of a bankruptcy or of a strategic takeover by another firm, such as a leveraged buyout by a private equity firm.

a. Net worth
b. Restructuring
c. Fair market value
d. Payback period

42. _____ are standards and interpretations adopted by the International Accounting Standards Board (IASB.)

Many of the standards forming part of _____ are known by the older name of International Accounting Standards (IAS.) IAS were issued between 1973 and 2001 by the board of the International Accounting Standards Committee (IASC.)

a. AIG
b. Out-of-pocket
c. ABC Television Network
d. International Financial Reporting Standards

43. The Federal National Mortgage Association (FNMA) (NYSE: FNM), commonly known as _____, is a stockholder-owned corporation chartered by Congress in 1968 as a government sponsored enterprise (GSE), but founded in 1938 during the Great Depression. The corporation's purpose is to purchase and securitize mortgages in order to ensure that funds are consistently available to the institutions that lend money to home buyers.

On September 7, 2008, James Lockhart, director of the Federal Housing Finance Agency (FHFA), announced that _____ and Freddie Mac were being placed into conservatorship of the FHFA.

a. National Conference of Commissioners on Uniform State Laws
b. Public company
c. Freddie Mac
d. Fannie Mae

44. _____ is one of a series of accounting transactions dealing with the billing of customers who owe money to a person, company or organization for goods and services that have been provided to the customer. In most business entities this is typically done by generating an invoice and mailing or electronically delivering it to the customer, who in turn must pay it within an established timeframe called credit or payment terms.

An example of a common payment term is Net 30, meaning payment is due in the amount of the invoice 30 days from the date of invoice.

a. Adjusting entries
b. Accrued revenue
c. Accrual
d. Accounts receivable

45. _____ represents claims for which formal instruments of credit are issued as evidence of debt, such as a promissory note. The credit instrument normally requires the debtor to pay interest and extends for time periods of 60-90 days or longer.

   a. Notes receivable
   b. Public offering
   c. Restricted stock
   d. Moving average

46. A _____ is a social, economic, theological, spiritual, scientific or legal issue which has become a political issue, as a result of deliberate action or otherwise, whereby people become politically active over that issue.

A contemporary example is abortion, an emotive and moral issue which has become a highly contentious legal and political issue in many countries. Terminology relating to such issues often takes the form of loaded language which contrasts with the pejorative terms used in reference to opponents.

   a. Cost the limit of price
   b. BMC Software, Inc.
   c. 3M Company
   d. Politicized issue

Chapter 2. Conceptual Framework Underlying Financial Accounting,

1. _____ were published by Accounting Principles Board (APB.) The board was created by American Institute of Certified Public Accountants (AICPA) in 1959 and was replaced by Financial Accounting Standards Board (FASB) in 1973. Its mission was to develop an overall conceptual framework of US generally accepted accounting principles (US GAAP.)
   a. ABC Television Network
   b. AIG
   c. AMEX
   d. Accounting Principles Board Opinions

2. The _____ founded on April 1, 2001 is the successor of the International Accounting Standards Committee (IASC) founded in June 1973 in London. It is responsible for developing the International Financial Reporting Standards (new name for the International Accounting Standards issued after 2001), and promoting the use and application of these standards.

   The _____ is an independent, privately-funded accounting standard-setter based in London, UK.

   a. Institute of Management Accountants
   b. Emerging technologies
   c. International Accounting Standards Board
   d. Information Systems Audit and Control Association

3. In economics, business, retail, and accounting, a _____ is the value of money that has been used up to produce something, and hence is not available for use anymore. In economics, a _____ is an alternative that is given up as a result of a decision. In business, the _____ may be one of acquisition, in which case the amount of money expended to acquire it is counted as _____.
   a. Cost
   b. Cost of quality
   c. Cost allocation
   d. Prime cost

4. The _____ is a private, not-for-profit organization whose primary purpose is to develop generally accepted accounting principles (GAAP) within the United States in the public's interest. The Securities and Exchange Commission (SEC) designated the _____ as the organization responsible for setting accounting standards for public companies in the U.S. It was created in 1973, replacing the Accounting Principles Board and the Committee on Accounting Procedure of the American Institute of Certified Public Accountants. The _____'s mission is 'to establish and improve standards of financial accounting and reporting for the guidance and education of the public, including issuers, auditors, and users of financial information.'

   The _____ is not a governmental body.

   a. Governmental Accounting Standards Board
   b. Fannie Mae
   c. Public company
   d. Financial Accounting Standards Board

5. In financial accounting, a _____ is defined as an obligation of an entity arising from past transactions or events, the settlement of which may result in the transfer or use of assets, provision of services or other yielding of economic benefits in the future.
   a. False Claims Act
   b. Vested
   c. Corporate governance
   d. Liability

6. The _____ is the current method of accelerated asset depreciation required by the United States income tax code. Under _____, all assets are divided into classes which dictate the number of years over which an asset's cost will be recovered.

Prior to the Accelerated Cost Recovery System (ACRS), most capital purchases were depreciated using a straight line technique, that allowed for the depreciation of the asset over its useful life.

Chapter 2. Conceptual Framework Underlying Financial Accounting,

a. 3M Company
c. Categorical grants

b. BMC Software, Inc.
d. Modified Accelerated Cost Recovery System

7. In economic models, the _____ time frame assumes no fixed factors of production. Firms can enter or leave the marketplace, and the cost (and availability) of land, labor, raw materials, and capital goods can be assumed to vary. In contrast, in the short-run time frame, certain factors are assumed to be fixed, because there is not sufficient time for them to change.

a. Short-run
c. BMC Software, Inc.

b. 3M Company
d. Long-run

8. _____ is that which is owed; usually referencing assets owed, but the term can also cover moral obligations and other interactions not requiring money. In the case of assets, _____ is a means of using future purchasing power in the present before a summation has been earned. Some companies and corporations use _____ as a part of their overall corporate finance strategy.

a. Lender
c. Debt

b. Debenture
d. Loan

9. Procter is a surname, and may also refer to:

- Bryan Waller Procter (pseud. Barry Cornwall), English poet
- Goodwin Procter, American law firm
- _____, consumer products multinational

a. Markup
c. Welfare

b. Screening
d. Procter ' Gamble

Chapter 3. The Accounting Information System,

1. The _____ of 1977 (15 U.S.C. ÂÂ§ÂÂ§ 78dd-1, et seq.) is a United States federal law known primarily for two of its main provisions, one that addresses accounting transparency requirements under the Securities Exchange Act of 1934 and another concerning bribery of foreign officials.
   a. Foreign Corrupt Practices Act
   b. Pre-emption right
   c. Competition law
   d. Lease

2. An _____ is a term used in behavioral economics to describe those types of behaviors that impose costs on a person in the long-run that are not taken into account when making decisions in the present. Classical Economics discourages government from creating legislation that targets internalities, because it is assumed that the consumer takes these personal costs into account when paying for the good that causes the _____. For example, cigarettes should be taxed because of the negative consumption externalities that they impose, such as second-hand smoke, not because the smoker harms him or herself by smoking.
   a. Inventory turnover ratio
   b. Operating budget
   c. Authorised capital
   d. Internality

3. The _____ is the United States federal government agency that collects taxes and enforces the internal revenue laws. It is an agency within the U.S. Dept of the treasury responsible for interpretation and application of Federal tax law. The official U.S. Treasury regulations provide (in part):

The _____ is a bureau of the Department of the Treasury under the immediate direction of the Commissioner of Internal Revenue.

   a. Use tax
   b. Internal Revenue Service
   c. Indirect tax
   d. Income tax

4. An _____ invented by esteemed professor Karen Osterheld is the system of records a business keeps to maintain its accounting system. This includes the purchase, sales, and other financial processes of the business. The purpose of an _____ is to accumulate data and provide decision makers (investors, creditors, and managers) with information to make decision While this was previously a paper-based process, most modern businesses now use accounting software such as UBS, MYOB etc.
   a. Accounting information system
   b. AIG
   c. AMEX
   d. ABC Television Network

5. In accounting, the _____ is a worksheet listing the balance at a certain date, of each ledger account in two columns, namely debit and credit. Under the double-entry system, in any transaction the total of any debits must equal the total of any credits, so in a _____ the total of the debit side should always be equal to the total of the credit side. The _____ thus serves as a tool to detect errors, which can result in the totals not being equal.
   a. Bottom line
   b. Depreciation
   c. Current asset
   d. Trial balance

6. In financial accounting, a _____ or statement of financial position is a summary of a person's or organization's balances. Assets, liabilities and ownership equity are listed as of a specific date, such as the end of its financial year. A _____ is often described as a snapshot of a company's financial condition.

a. Financial statements
b. Balance sheet
c. 3M Company
d. Statement of retained earnings

7. _____ is the recording of the value of assets, liabilities, income, and expenses in the daybooks, journals, and ledgers, in which debit and credit entries are chronologically posted to record changes in value. _____ is often mistaken for accounting, which is the system of recording, verifying, and reporting such information. Practitioners of accounting are called accountants.

a. Debit and credit
b. Bookkeeping
c. Double-entry bookkeeping
d. Controlling account

8. The _____, sometimes known as the nominal ledger, is the main accounting record of a business which uses double-entry bookkeeping. It will usually include accounts for such items as current assets, fixed assets, liabilities, revenue and expense items, gains and losses.

The _____ is a collection of the group of accounts that supports the items shown in the major financial statements.

a. Sales journal
b. General ledger
c. General journal
d. Journal entry

9. A _____ has several related meanings:

- a daily record of events or business; a private _____ is usually referred to as a diary.
- a newspaper or other periodical, in the literal sense of one published each day;
- many publications issued at stated intervals, such as magazines, or scholarly academic _____s, or the record of the transactions of a society, are often called _____s. Although _____ is sometimes used, erroneously, as a synonym for 'magazine,' in academic use, a _____ refers to a serious, scholarly publication, most often peer-reviewed. A non-scholarly magazine written for an educated audience about an industry or an area of professional activity is usually called a professional magazine.

The word 'journalist' for one whose business is writing for the public press has been in use since the end of the 17th century.

Open access _____s are scholarly _____s that are available to the reader without financial or other barrier other than access to the internet itself. Some are subsidized, and some require payment on behalf of the author. Subsidized _____s are financed by an academic institution or a government information center.

a. BMC Software, Inc.
b. 3M Company
c. BNSF Railway
d. Journal

10. A _____, in business matters, is an entity that is controlled by a bigger and more powerful entity. The controlled entity is called a company, corporation, or limited liability company, and the controlling entity is called its parent (or the parent company.) The reason for this distinction is that a lone company cannot be a _____ of any organization; only an entity representing a legal fiction as a separate entity can be a _____.

Chapter 3. The Accounting Information System,

a. Parent company
b. BMC Software, Inc.
c. 3M Company
d. Subsidiary

11. The _____ is a subset of the general ledger used in accounting. The _____ shows detail for part of the accounting records such as property and equipment, prepaid expenses, etc. The detail would include such items as date the item was purchased or expense incurred, a description of the item, the original balance, and the net book value.
   a. Remittance advice
   b. Credit memo
   c. Minority interest
   d. Subledger

12. _____ are journal entries made at the end of an accounting period to transfer temporary accounts to permanent accounts. An 'income summary' account may be used to show the balance between revenue and expenses, or they could be directly closed against retained earnings where dividend payments will be deducted from. This process is used to reset the balance of these temporary accounts to zero for the next accounting period.
   a. FIFO and LIFO accounting
   b. Trial balance
   c. Treasury stock
   d. Closing entries

13. _____ and credit are formal bookkeeping and accounting terms. They are the most fundamental concepts in accounting, representing the two records that one party in a transaction makes on its records, transferring a money balance from one account to another, one representing a reduction of liability or increase in asset, and the other representing a balancing increase in liability or reduction of asset.

Introduction

_____s and credits are a system of notation used in accounting to keep track of money movements (transactions) into and out of an account.

   a. Debit and credit
   b. Bookkeeping
   c. Cookie jar accounting
   d. Debit

14. _____ is a system of financial accounting where each transaction is recorded in at least two accounts: at least one account is debited and at least one account is credited, so that the total debits of the transaction equal to the total credits. For example, if Company A sells an item to Company B, and Company B pays by cheque, then the bookkeeper of Company A credits the account 'Sales' and debits the account 'Bank'. Conversely, the bookkeeper of Company B debits the account 'Purchases' and credits the account 'Bank'.
   a. Debit and credit
   b. Bookkeeping
   c. Cookie jar accounting
   d. Double-entry bookkeeping

15. The _____ is a private, not-for-profit organization whose primary purpose is to develop generally accepted accounting principles (GAAP) within the United States in the public's interest. The Securities and Exchange Commission (SEC) designated the _____ as the organization responsible for setting accounting standards for public companies in the U.S. It was created in 1973, replacing the Accounting Principles Board and the Committee on Accounting Procedure of the American Institute of Certified Public Accountants. The _____'s mission is 'to establish and improve standards of financial accounting and reporting for the guidance and education of the public, including issuers, auditors, and users of financial information.'

The _____ is not a governmental body.

a. Public company
c. Fannie Mae
b. Governmental Accounting Standards Board
d. Financial Accounting Standards Board

16. _____ is a company's financial statement that indicates how the revenue is transformed into the net income The purpose of the _____ is to show managers and investors whether the company made or lost money during the period being reported.

The important thing to remember about an _____ is that it represents a period of time.

a. AIG
c. Income statement
b. ABC Television Network
d. AMEX

17. In financial accounting, a _____ or Statement of cash flows is a financial statement that shows a company's flow of cash. The money coming into the business is called cash inflow, and money going out from the business is called cash outflow. The statement shows how changes in balance sheet and income accounts affect cash and cash equivalents, and breaks the analysis down to operating, investing, and financing activities.

a. Cash flow statement
c. BMC Software, Inc.
b. BNSF Railway
d. 3M Company

18. _____ is the balance of the amounts of cash being received and paid by a business during a defined period of time, sometimes tied to a specific project. Measurement of _____ can be used

- to evaluate the state or performance of a business or project.
- to determine problems with liquidity. Being profitable does not necessarily mean being liquid. A company can fail because of a shortage of cash, even while profitable.
- to project rate of returns. The time of _____s into and out of projects are used as inputs to financial models such as internal rate of return, and net present value.
- to examine income or growth of a business when it is believed that accrual accounting concepts do not represent economic realities. Alternately, _____ can be used to 'validate' the net income generated by accrual accounting.

_____ as a generic term may be used differently depending on context, and certain _____ definitions may be adapted by analysts and users for their own uses. Common terms include operating _____ and free _____.

a. Cash flow
c. Commercial paper
b. Flow-through entity
d. Controlling interest

19. _____ is the state or fact of exclusive rights and control over property, which may be an object, land/real estate or intellectual property. An _____ right is also referred to as title.

_____ is the key building block in the development of the capitalist socio-economic system.

a. Administrative proceeding
c. ABC Television Network
b. Ownership
d. Encumbrance

Chapter 3. The Accounting Information System,

20. The Exxon Mobil Corporation is an American oil and gas corporation. It is a direct descendant of John D. Rockefeller's Standard Oil company, formed on November 30, 1999, by the merger of Exxon and Mobil.

_____ is the world's largest publicly traded company when measured by either revenue or market capitalization.

a. Alan Greenspan
c. Arthur Betz Laffer
b. Abby Joseph Cohen
d. ExxonMobil

21. The term _____, derived from the distinctive T shape, is frequently used when discussing or analyzing accounting or business transactions. _____s are used to represent general ledger accounts.

Typically one or more Ts are drawn on a white board or blank piece of paper. A general ledger account name or number is then written above each T. Debit entries are recorded on the left side of the 'T' and credit entries are recorded on the right side of the 'T'.

a. T account
c. BNSF Railway
b. 3M Company
d. BMC Software, Inc.

22. _____ means the giving out of information, either voluntarily or to be in compliance with legal regulations or workplace rules.

- In Computer security, full _____ means disclosing full information about vulnerabilities.
- In computing, _____ widget
- Journalism, full _____ refers to disclosing the interests of the writer which may bear on the subject being written about, for example, if the writer has worked with an interview subject in the past.

- In law:
    - The law of England and Wales, _____ refers to a process that may form part of legal proceedings, whereby parties inform to other parties the existence of any relevant documents that are, or have been, in their control. This compares with the process known as discovery in the course of legal proceedings in the United States.
    - In U.S. civil procedure (litigation rules for civil cases), _____ is a stage prior to trial. In civil cases, each party must disclose to the opposing party the following: names of witnesses which it may use to support its side, copies of documents (or mere description of these documents) in its control which it may use to support its side, computation of damages claimed, and certain insurance information. _____ is related to, but technically prior to, the discovery stage.
    - In Company law (known as 'corporate law' in the United States), _____ refers to giving out information about public or limited companies or their officers, which might be kept secret if the company was a private company or a partnership.

- In real property transactions, _____ refers to providing to a buyer information known to the seller or broker/agent concerning the condition or other aspects of real property that would affect the property's value or desirability. These rules regarding what information must be disclosed, and whether the information must be disclosed even if a buyer does not ask, vary from one jurisdiction to the next.

Chapter 3. The Accounting Information System,

a. Controlled Foreign Corporations
b. Tax harmonisation
c. Trailing
d. Disclosure

23. The _____ is where double entry bookkeeping entries are recorded by debiting one account and crediting another account with the same amount. The amount debited and the amount credited should always be equal, thereby ensuring the accounting equation is maintained.

Depending on the business's accounting information system, specialized journals may be used in conjunction with the _____ for record-keeping.

a. General ledger
b. Sales journal
c. Journal entry
d. General journal

24. A _____, in accounting, is a logging of transcriptions into items accounting journal. The _____ can consist of several items, each of which is either a debit or a credit. The total of the debits must equal the total of the credits, or the _____ is said to be 'unbalanced.' Journal entries can record unique items or recurring items such as depreciation or bond amortization.

a. General ledger
b. Sales journal
c. General journal
d. Journal entry

25. _____ of something is, in finance, the adding together of interest or different investments over a period of time such as atoms (1 - the act or process of accruing; 2 - the amount that accrues.) It holds specific meanings in accounting and payroll.

_____, in accounting, describes the accounting method known as _____ basis, whereby revenues and expenses are recognized when they are accrued, i.e. accumulated (earned or incurred), regardless when the actual cash is received or paid out.

a. Accounts receivable
b. Earnings before interest, taxes, depreciation and amortization
c. Assets
d. Accrual

26. _____, is a liability with an uncertain timing or amount, but where the uncertainty is not significant enough to qualify it as a provision. An example is an unpaid obligation to pay for goods or services received FROM a counterpart, while cash for them is to be paid out in a latter accounting period when its amount is deducted from _____s.

a. Accounts receivable
b. Accrued expense
c. Assets
d. Accrual basis accounting

27. _____ is an asset, such as unpaid proceeds from a delivery of goods or services, at which such income item is earned and the related revenue item is recognized, while cash for them is to be received in a latter period, when its amount is deducted from the _____.

a. Assets
b. Accrued expense
c. Accounts receivable
d. Accrued revenue

Chapter 3. The Accounting Information System,

28. _____ refers to services paid for in advance. Examples include tolls, pay as you go cell phones, and stored-value cards such as gift cards and preloaded credit cards. _____ accounts are assets, and they are increased by debiting the account(s.)
   a. BMC Software, Inc.
   b. BNSF Railway
   c. Prepaid
   d. 3M Company

29. _____, in accrual accounting, is any account where the asset or liability is not realized until a future date (accounting period), e.g. annuities, charges, taxes, income, etc. The _____ item may be carried, dependent on type of deferral, as either an asset or liability.
   a. Pro forma
   b. Deferred
   c. Cash basis accounting
   d. Payroll

30. _____, in accrual accounting, (e.g. advance payment received from a client) is, according to revenue recognition, revenue not earned until the delivery of goods or services, which until then, is still owed to the payer, hence remaining a liability.

_____, sometimes referred to as deferred revenue or unearned revenue, shares characteristics with accrued expense with the difference that a liability to be covered latter is cash received FROM a counterpart, while goods or services are to be delivered in a latter period, when such income item is earned, the related revenue item is recognized, and the same amount is deducted from deferred revenues.

   a. Gross sales
   b. Treasury stock
   c. Deferred income
   d. Matching principle

31. In accounting/accountancy, _____ are journal entries usually made at the end of an accounting period to allocate income and expenditure to the period in which they actually occurred. The revenue recognition principle is the basis of making _____ that pertain to unearned and accrued revenues under accrual-basis accounting. They are sometimes called Balance Day adjustments because they are made on balance day.
   a. Accrual
   b. Earnings before interest, taxes, depreciation and amortization
   c. Accrued expense
   d. Adjusting entries

32. In accounting, _____ has a very specific meaning. It is an outflow of cash or other valuable assets from a person or company to another person or company. This outflow of cash is generally one side of a trade for products or services that have equal or better current or future value to the buyer than to the seller.
   a. AMEX
   b. AIG
   c. ABC Television Network
   d. Expense

33. _____, in law and economics, is a form of risk management primarily used to hedge against the risk of a contingent loss. _____ is defined as the equitable transfer of the risk of a loss, from one entity to another, in exchange for a premium, and can be thought of as a guaranteed small loss to prevent a large, possibly devastating loss. An insurer is a company selling the _____; an insured is the person or entity buying the _____.
   a. ABC Television Network
   b. AIG
   c. AMEX
   d. Insurance

34. Book Value = Original Cost - _____

Book value at the end of year becomes book value at the beginning of next year. The asset is depreciated until the book value equals scrap value.

If the vehicle were to be sold and the sales price exceeded the depreciated value (net book value) then the excess would be considered a gain and subject to depreciation recapture.

a. AMEX
b. ABC Television Network
c. AIG
d. Accumulated Depreciation

35. In finance, a _____ is a type of bond that can be converted into shares of stock in the issuing company, usually at some pre-announced ratio. It is a hybrid security with debt- and equity-like features. Although it typically has a low coupon rate, the holder is compensated with the ability to convert the bond to common stock, usually at a substantial discount to the stock's market value.
a. Coupon rate
b. Zero-coupon bond
c. Zero-coupon
d. Convertible bond

36. _____ is that which is owed; usually referencing assets owed, but the term can also cover moral obligations and other interactions not requiring money. In the case of assets, _____ is a means of using future purchasing power in the present before a summation has been earned. Some companies and corporations use _____ as a part of their overall corporate finance strategy.
a. Lender
b. Loan
c. Debenture
d. Debt

37. _____ is a term used in accounting, economics and finance to spread the cost of an asset over the span of several years.

In simple words we can say that _____ is the reduction in the value of an asset due to usage, passage of time, wear and tear, technological outdating or obsolescence, depletion, inadequacy, rot, rust, decay or other such factors.

In accounting, _____ is a term used to describe any method of attributing the historical or purchase cost of an asset across its useful life, roughly corresponding to normal wear and tear.

a. Current asset
b. Net profit
c. Depreciation
d. General ledger

38. In economic models, the _____ time frame assumes no fixed factors of production. Firms can enter or leave the marketplace, and the cost (and availability) of land, labor, raw materials, and capital goods can be assumed to vary. In contrast, in the short-run time frame, certain factors are assumed to be fixed, because there is not sufficient time for them to change.
a. Long-run
b. BMC Software, Inc.
c. 3M Company
d. Short-run

39. In accounting, _____ or carrying value is the value of an asset according to its balance sheet account balance. For assets, the value is based on the original cost of the asset less any depreciation, amortization or impairment costs made against the asset. Traditionally, a company's _____ is its total assets minus intangible assets and liabilities.

   a. Matching principle
   b. Generally accepted accounting principles
   c. Book value
   d. Depreciation

40. In finance, _____ is the interest that has accumulated since the principal investment, or since the previous interest payment if there has been one already. For a financial instrument such as a bond, interest is calculated and paid in set intervals.

The primary formula for calculating the interest accrued in a given period is:

$$I_A = T \times P \times R$$

where I_A is the _____, T is the fraction of the year, P is the principal, and R is the annualized interest rate.

   a. Accrued interest
   b. AIG
   c. Interest
   d. ABC Television Network

41. _____ is a fee paid on borrowed assets. It is the price paid for the use of borrowed money, or, money earned by deposited funds. Assets that are sometimes lent with _____ include money, shares, consumer goods through hire purchase, major assets such as aircraft, and even entire factories in finance lease arrangements. The _____ is calculated upon the value of the assets in the same manner as upon money.

   a. AIG
   b. ABC Television Network
   c. Insolvency
   d. Interest

42. In financial accounting and finance, _____ is the portion of receivables that can no longer be collected, typically from accounts receivable or loans. _____ in accounting is considered an expense.

There are two methods to account for _____:

   1. Direct write off method (Non - GAAP)

A receivable which is not considered collectible is charged directly to the income statement.

   1. Allowance method (GAAP)

An estimate is made at the end of each fiscal year of the amount of _____. This is then accumulated in a provision which is then used to reduce specific receivable accounts as and when necessary.

   a. 3M Company
   b. Total Expense Ratio
   c. Tax expense
   d. Bad debt

43. _____ are formal records of a business' financial activities.

In British English, including United Kingdom company law, _____ are often referred to as accounts, although the term _____ is also used, particularly by accountants.

_____ provide an overview of a business' financial condition in both short and long term.

a. 3M Company
b. Notes to the financial statements
c. Statement of retained earnings
d. Financial statements

44. _____, also called fair price (in a commonplace conflation of the two distinct concepts), is a concept used in finance and economics, defined as a rational and unbiased estimate of the potential market price of a good, service, or asset, taking into account such objective factors as:

- acquisition/production/distribution costs, replacement costs, or costs of close substitutes
- actual utility at a given level of development of social productive capability
- supply vs. demand

and subjective factors such as

- risk characteristics
- cost of capital
- individually perceived utility

In accounting, _____ is used as an estimate of the market value of an asset (or liability) for which a market price cannot be determined (usually because there is no established market for the asset.) Under GAAP (FAS 157), _____ is the amount at which the asset could be bought or sold in a current transaction between willing parties, or transferred to an equivalent party, other than in a liquidation sale. This is used for assets whose carrying value is based on mark-to-market valuations; for assets carried at historical cost, the _____ of the asset is not used. One example of where _____ is an issue is a College kitchen with a cost of $2 million which was built 5 years ago.

a. BNSF Railway
b. BMC Software, Inc.
c. 3M Company
d. Fair value

45. In business and accounting, _____ are everything of value that is owned by a person or company. It is a claim on the property your income of a borrower. The balance sheet of a firm records the monetary value of the _____ owned by the firm.

a. Accrual basis accounting
b. Earnings before interest, taxes, depreciation and amortization
c. Accounts receivable
d. Assets

46. _____ in economics and business is the result of an exchange and from that trade we assign a numerical monetary value to a good, service or asset. If Alice trades Bob 4 apples for an orange, the _____ of an orange is 4 apples. Inversely, the _____ of an apple is 1/4 oranges.

Chapter 3. The Accounting Information System,

a. Price
b. Transactional Net Margin Method
c. Price discrimination
d. Discounts and allowances

47. _____ refers to the methods, practices and operations conducted to promote and sustain certain categories of commercial activity. The term is understood to have different specific meanings depending on the context. Merchandise is a sale goods at a store

In marketing, one of the definitions of _____ is the practice in which the brand or image from one product or service is used to sell another.

a. BMC Software, Inc.
b. 3M Company
c. Merchandise
d. Merchandising

48. The _____ is one of the basic financial statements as per Generally Accepted Accounting Principles, and it explains the changes in a company's retained earnings over the reporting period. It breaks down changes affecting the account, such as profits or losses from operations, dividends paid, and any other items charged or credited to retained earnings. A retained earnings statement is required by Generally Accepted Accounting Principles whenever comparative balance sheets and income statements are presented.

a. 3M Company
b. Statement of retained earnings
c. Financial statements
d. Notes to the financial statements

49. _____ is a specific term used in companies' financial reporting from the company-whole point of view. Because that use excludes the effects of changing ownership interest, an economic measure of _____ is necessary for financial analysis from the shareholders' point of view

_____ is defined by the Financial Accounting Standards Board, or FASB, as 'the change in equity [net assets] of a business enterprise during a period from transactions and other events and circumstances from nonowner sources. It includes all changes in equity during a period except those resulting from investments by owners and distributions to owners.'

_____ is the sum of net income and other items that must bypass the income statement because they have not been realized, including items like an unrealized holding gain or loss from available for sale securities and foreign currency translation gains or losses.

a. 3M Company
b. Comprehensive income
c. BNSF Railway
d. BMC Software, Inc.

50. In economics, business, retail, and accounting, a _____ is the value of money that has been used up to produce something, and hence is not available for use anymore. In economics, a _____ is an alternative that is given up as a result of a decision. In business, the _____ may be one of acquisition, in which case the amount of money expended to acquire it is counted as _____.

a. Cost of quality
b. Cost allocation
c. Prime cost
d. Cost

Chapter 3. The Accounting Information System,

51. In financial accounting, _____ or cost of sales includes the direct costs attributable to the production of the goods sold by a company. This amount includes the materials cost used in creating the goods along with the direct labor costs used to produce the good. It excludes indirect expenses such as distribution costs and sales force costs.
   a. FIFO and LIFO accounting
   b. Reorder point
   c. 3M Company
   d. Cost of goods sold

52. _____ is a method of accounting whereby economic activities (rather than cash flow) of financial events are considered, because of two complementary principles, which (together) determine the point, at which expenses and revenues are recognized. According to revenue recognition principle, revenues are realized when earned, whether or not they are received in cash.
   a. Accrued revenue
   b. Earnings before interest, taxes, depreciation and amortization
   c. Accrual
   d. Accrual basis accounting

53. _____ is a method of accounting whereby cash flow of financial events is considered. The method recognizes revenues when cash is received and recognizes expenses when cash is paid out. In cash accounting, revenues and expenses are also called cash receipts and cash payments respectively.
   a. Closing entries
   b. Treasury stock
   c. Net sales
   d. Cash basis accounting

54. An _____, operating expenditure, operational expense, operational expenditure or OPEX is an on-going cost for running a product, business, or system. Its counterpart, a capital expenditure (CAPEX), is the cost of developing or providing non-consumable parts for the product or system. For example, the purchase of a photocopier is the CAPEX, and the annual paper and toner cost is the OPEX.
   a. ABC Television Network
   b. AMEX
   c. AIG
   d. Operating expense

55. A _____ is a piece of paper, often preprinted in a way designed to help organize material for learning or clear understanding. Students in a school may have 'fill-in-the-blank' sheets of questions, diagrams or maps to help them with their exercises. Students will often use _____ s to review what has been taught in class.
   a. Worksheet
   b. Value based pricing
   c. BMC Software, Inc.
   d. 3M Company

56. Procter is a surname, and may also refer to:

   - Bryan Waller Procter (pseud. Barry Cornwall), English poet
   - Goodwin Procter, American law firm
   - _____, consumer products multinational

   a. Screening
   b. Welfare
   c. Markup
   d. Procter ' Gamble

57. A _____ is a type of debt Like all debt instruments, a _____ entails the redistribution of financial assets over time, between the lender and the borrower.

a. Loan
c. Loan to value
b. Lender
d. Debenture

Chapter 4. Income Statement and Related Information,

1. The term _____ is a term applied to practices that are perfunctory, or seek to satisfy the minimum requirements or to conform to a convention or doctrine. It has different meanings in different fields.

In accounting, _____ earnings are those earnings of companies in addition to actual earnings calculated under the Generally Accepted Accounting Principles (GAAP) in their quarterly and yearly financial reports.

   a. Pro forma
   b. Bottom line
   c. Treasury stock
   d. Payroll

2. A _____ is a fungible, negotiable instrument representing financial value. they are broadly categorized into debt securities (such as banknotes, bonds and debentures), and equity securities; e.g., common stocks. The company or other entity issuing the _____ is called the issuer.
   a. Tracking stock
   b. BMC Software, Inc.
   c. 3M Company
   d. Security

3. The U.S. _____ is an independent agency of the United States government which holds primary responsibility for enforcing the federal securities laws and regulating the securities industry, the nation's stock and options exchanges, and other electronic securities markets. The SEC was created by section 4 of the Securities Exchange Act of 1934 (now codified as 15 U.S.C. ÂÂ§ 78d and commonly referred to as the 1934 Act.)
   a. 3M Company
   b. Securities and Exchange Commission
   c. BNSF Railway
   d. BMC Software, Inc.

4. _____ is a specific term used in companies' financial reporting from the company-whole point of view. Because that use excludes the effects of changing ownership interest, an economic measure of _____ is necessary for financial analysis from the shareholders' point of view

_____ is defined by the Financial Accounting Standards Board, or FASB, as 'the change in equity [net assets] of a business enterprise during a period from transactions and other events and circumstances from nonowner sources. It includes all changes in equity during a period except those resulting from investments by owners and distributions to owners.'

_____ is the sum of net income and other items that must bypass the income statement because they have not been realized, including items like an unrealized holding gain or loss from available for sale securities and foreign currency translation gains or losses.

   a. 3M Company
   b. Comprehensive income
   c. BNSF Railway
   d. BMC Software, Inc.

5. _____ is a company's financial statement that indicates how the revenue is transformed into the net income The purpose of the _____ is to show managers and investors whether the company made or lost money during the period being reported.

The important thing to remember about an _____ is that it represents a period of time.

   a. AIG
   b. ABC Television Network
   c. AMEX
   d. Income statement

Chapter 4. Income Statement and Related Information,

6. The _____ founded on April 1, 2001 is the successor of the International Accounting Standards Committee (IASC) founded in June 1973 in London. It is responsible for developing the International Financial Reporting Standards (new name for the International Accounting Standards issued after 2001), and promoting the use and application of these standards.

The _____ is an independent, privately-funded accounting standard-setter based in London, UK.

- a. Emerging technologies
- b. International Accounting Standards Board
- c. Institute of Management Accountants
- d. Information Systems Audit and Control Association

7. _____ or cookie jar reserves is an accounting practice in which a company uses generous reserves from good years against losses that might be incurred in bad years.

An example of a cookie jar reserve is a liability created when a company records an expense that is not directly linked to a specific accounting period -- the expense may fall in one period or another. Companies may record such discretionary expense when profits are high because they can afford to take the hit to income.

- a. Cookie jar accounting
- b. Controlling account
- c. Debit and credit
- d. Bookkeeping

8. Creative accounting and _____ are euphemisms referring to accounting practices that may follow the letter of the rules of standard accounting practices, but certainly deviate from the spirit of those rules. They are characterized by excessive complication and the use of novel ways of characterizing income, assets, or liabilities and the intent to influence readers towards the interpretations desired by the authors. The terms 'innovative' or 'aggressive' are also sometimes used.

- a. ABC Television Network
- b. AMEX
- c. Earnings management
- d. AIG

9. _____ are the earnings returned on the initial investment amount.

In the US, the Financial Accounting Standards Board (FASB) requires companies' income statements to report _____ for each of the major categories of the income statement: continuing operations, discontinued operations, extraordinary items, and net income.

The _____ formula does not include preferred dividends for categories outside of continued operations and net income.

- a. Average accounting return
- b. Earnings yield
- c. Invested capital
- d. Earnings per share

10. A _____ is any one of a variety of different systems, institutions, procedures, social relations and infrastructures whereby persons trade, and goods and services are exchanged, forming part of the economy. It is an arrangement that allows buyers and sellers to exchange things. _____s vary in size, range, geographic scale, location, types and variety of human communities, as well as the types of goods and services traded.

- a. Market Failure
- b. Recession
- c. Market
- d. Perfect competition

Chapter 4. Income Statement and Related Information,

11. _____ is the price at which an asset would trade in a competitive Walrasian auction setting. _____ is often used interchangeably with open _____, fair value or fair _____, although these terms have distinct definitions in different standards, and may differ in some circumstances.

International Valuation Standards defines _____ as 'the estimated amount for which a property should exchange on the date of valuation between a willing buyer and a willing seller in an arme;s-length transaction after proper marketing wherein the parties had each acted knowledgeably, prudently, and without compulsion.'

_____ is a concept distinct from market price, which is e;the price at which one can transacte;, while _____ is e;the true underlying valuee; according to theoretical standards.

   a. Debtor
   b. Market value
   c. Segregated portfolio company
   d. Sinking fund

12. _____ is a business intelligence (BI), enterprise reporting, and OLAP (on-line analytical processing) software vendor. _____'s software allows reporting and analysis of data stored in a relational database, multidimensional database, or flat data file. _____ describes its core reporting software as having a 'ROLAP' or 'Relational OLAP' architecture, meaning that a complex relational database can be expressed using a virtual multidimensional cube structure that can be more easily understood by business users who wish to navigate through the data.
   a. MicroStrategy
   b. Financial Accounting Standards Board
   c. Professional association
   d. Privately held

13. In accounting, _____ has a very specific meaning. It is an outflow of cash or other valuable assets from a person or company to another person or company. This outflow of cash is generally one side of a trade for products or services that have equal or better current or future value to the buyer than to the seller.
   a. AIG
   b. Expense
   c. AMEX
   d. ABC Television Network

14. _____ are formal records of a business' financial activities.

In British English, including United Kingdom company law, _____ are often referred to as accounts, although the term _____ is also used, particularly by accountants.

_____ provide an overview of a business' financial condition in both short and long term.

   a. Financial Statements
   b. Notes to the financial statements
   c. 3M Company
   d. Statement of retained earnings

15. _____ were published by Accounting Principles Board (APB.) The board was created by American Institute of Certified Public Accountants (AICPA) in 1959 and was replaced by Financial Accounting Standards Board (FASB) in 1973. Its mission was to develop an overall conceptual framework of US generally accepted accounting principles (US GAAP.)
   a. ABC Television Network
   b. AMEX
   c. AIG
   d. Accounting Principles Board Opinions

Chapter 4. Income Statement and Related Information,

16. In economics, business, retail, and accounting, a _____ is the value of money that has been used up to produce something, and hence is not available for use anymore. In economics, a _____ is an alternative that is given up as a result of a decision. In business, the _____ may be one of acquisition, in which case the amount of money expended to acquire it is counted as _____.

   a. Cost allocation
   b. Prime cost
   c. Cost of quality
   d. Cost

17. In financial accounting, _____ or cost of sales includes the direct costs attributable to the production of the goods sold by a company. This amount includes the materials cost used in creating the goods along with the direct labor costs used to produce the good. It excludes indirect expenses such as distribution costs and sales force costs.

   a. FIFO and LIFO accounting
   b. 3M Company
   c. Cost of goods sold
   d. Reorder point

18. _____ is a term used with respect to a retailed product, indicating that the product is in the end of its product lifetime and a vendor will no longer be marketing, selling, or promoting a particular product and may also be limiting or ending support for the product. In the specific case of product sales, the term end-of-sale (EOS) has also been used. The term lifetime, after the last production date, depends on the product and is related to a customer's expected product lifetime.

   a. ABC Television Network
   b. AMEX
   c. AIG
   d. End-of-life

19. The _____ is a private, not-for-profit organization whose primary purpose is to develop generally accepted accounting principles (GAAP) within the United States in the public's interest. The Securities and Exchange Commission (SEC) designated the _____ as the organization responsible for setting accounting standards for public companies in the U.S. It was created in 1973, replacing the Accounting Principles Board and the Committee on Accounting Procedure of the American Institute of Certified Public Accountants. The _____'s mission is 'to establish and improve standards of financial accounting and reporting for the guidance and education of the public, including issuers, auditors, and users of financial information.'

The _____ is not a governmental body.

   a. Financial Accounting Standards Board
   b. Governmental Accounting Standards Board
   c. Fannie Mae
   d. Public company

20. The _____ is currently the source of generally accepted accounting principles (GAAP) used by State and Local governments in the [[United States of America]]. As with most of the entities involved in creating GAAP in the United States, it is a private, non-governmental organization.

The _____ is subject to oversight by the Financial Accounting Foundation (FAF), which selects the members of the _____ and the Financial Accounting Standards Board, and funds both organizations.

   a. Multinational corporation
   b. Fannie Mae
   c. National Conference of Commissioners on Uniform State Laws
   d. Governmental Accounting Standards Board

Chapter 4. Income Statement and Related Information,

21. The term _____ describes a reduction in recognized value. In accounting terminology, it refers to recognition of the reduced or zero value of an asset. In income tax statements, it refers to a reduction of taxable income as recognition of certain expenses required to produce the income.
    a. Salvage value
    b. Payroll
    c. Current asset
    d. Write-off

22. _____ is that which is owed; usually referencing assets owed, but the term can also cover moral obligations and other interactions not requiring money. In the case of assets, _____ is a means of using future purchasing power in the present before a summation has been earned. Some companies and corporations use _____ as a part of their overall corporate finance strategy.
    a. Lender
    b. Debenture
    c. Debt
    d. Loan

23. _____ is the corporate management term for the act of partially dismantling or otherwise reorganizing a company for the purpose of making it more profitable. Also known as corporate _____, debt _____ and financial _____.

    _____ is often done as part of a bankruptcy or of a strategic takeover by another firm, such as a leveraged buyout by a private equity firm.

    a. Net worth
    b. Restructuring
    c. Payback period
    d. Fair market value

24. _____ are defined as identifiable non-monetary assets that cannot be seen, touched or physically measured, which are created through time and/or effort and that are identifiable as a separate asset. There are two primary forms of intangibles - legal intangibles (such as trade secrets (e.g., customer lists), copyrights, patents, trademarks, and goodwill) and competitive intangibles (such as knowledge activities (know-how, knowledge), collaboration activities, leverage activities, and structural activities.) Legal intangibles are known under the generic term intellectual property and generate legal property rights defensible in a court of law.
    a. Overhead
    b. ABC Television Network
    c. AIG
    d. Intangible assets

25. In business and accounting, _____ are everything of value that is owned by a person or company. It is a claim on the property your income of a borrower. The balance sheet of a firm records the monetary value of the _____ owned by the firm.
    a. Earnings before interest, taxes, depreciation and amortization
    b. Accrual basis accounting
    c. Accounts receivable
    d. Assets

26. An _____ is a tax levied on the financial income of people, corporations, or other legal entities. Various _____ systems exist, with varying degrees of tax incidence. Income taxation can be progressive, proportional, or regressive.
    a. Ordinary income
    b. Individual Retirement Arrangement
    c. Implied level of government service
    d. Income tax

Chapter 4. Income Statement and Related Information, 31

27. _____ is a form of corporation equity ownership represented in the securities. It is a stock whose dividends are based on market fluctuations. It is dangerous in comparison to preferred shares and some other investment options, in that in the event of bankruptcy, _____ investors receive their funds after preferred stock holders, bondholders, creditors, etc. On the other hand, common shares on average perform better than preferred shares or bonds over time.
   a. Growth investing
   b. Stock split
   c. 3M Company
   d. Common stock

28. In financial accounting, a _____ or statement of financial position is a summary of a person's or organization's balances. Assets, liabilities and ownership equity are listed as of a specific date, such as the end of its financial year. A _____ is often described as a snapshot of a company's financial condition.
   a. Statement of retained earnings
   b. Financial statements
   c. 3M Company
   d. Balance sheet

29. _____ is a fee paid on borrowed assets. It is the price paid for the use of borrowed money , or, money earned by deposited funds .Assets that are sometimes lent with _____ include money, shares, consumer goods through hire purchase, major assets such as aircraft, and even entire factories in finance lease arrangements. The _____ is calculated upon the value of the assets in the same manner as upon money.
   a. AIG
   b. ABC Television Network
   c. Insolvency
   d. Interest

30. Procter is a surname, and may also refer to:

   - Bryan Waller Procter (pseud. Barry Cornwall), English poet
   - Goodwin Procter, American law firm
   - _____, consumer products multinational

   a. Welfare
   b. Procter ' Gamble
   c. Markup
   d. Screening

31. _____ (NYSE: DE) is an American corporation based in Moline, Illinois, and the leading manufacturer of agricultural machinery in the world. In 2008, it was listed as 102nd in the Fortune 500 ranking. Deere and Company agricultural products, usually sold under the John Deere name, include tractors, combine harvesters, balers, planters/seeders, ATVs and forestry equipment.
   a. Governmental Accounting Standards Board
   b. Deere ' Company
   c. Freddie Mac
   d. Professional association

32. _____ was founded in 1898 by Frank Seiberling. Today it is the third largest tire company in the world after Bridgestone and Michelin. Goodyear manufactures tires for automobiles, commercial trucks, light trucks, SUVs, race cars, airplanes, and heavy earth-mover machinery.
   a. Factor
   b. Trailing
   c. Fiscal
   d. The Goodyear Tire ' Rubber Company

Chapter 5. Balance Sheet and Statement of Cash Flows,

1. In economics, _____ or _____ goods or real _____ refers to factors of production used to create goods or services that are not themselves significantly consumed (though they may depreciate) in the production process. _____ goods may be acquired with money or financial _____. In finance and accounting, _____ generally refers to financial wealth, especially that used to start or maintain a business.

   a. Disclosure
   b. Vyborg Appeal
   c. Screening
   d. Capital

2. _____ is the term used to refer to the standard framework of guidelines for financial accounting used in any given jurisdiction. _____ includes the standards, conventions, and rules accountants follow in recording and summarizing transactions, and in the preparation of financial statements.

   Financial accounting information must be assembled and reported objectively.

   a. General ledger
   b. Current asset
   c. Long-term liabilities
   d. Generally accepted accounting principles

3. In financial accounting, a _____ or statement of financial position is a summary of a person's or organization's balances. Assets, liabilities and ownership equity are listed as of a specific date, such as the end of its financial year. A _____ is often described as a snapshot of a company's financial condition.

   a. 3M Company
   b. Balance sheet
   c. Statement of retained earnings
   d. Financial statements

4. _____ is a concept that denotes the precise probability of specific eventualities. Technically, the notion of _____ is independent from the notion of value and, as such, eventualities may have both beneficial and adverse consequences. However, in general usage the convention is to focus only on potential negative impact to some characteristic of value that may arise from a future event.

   a. Discount factor
   b. Risk
   c. Discounting
   d. Risk adjusted return on capital

5. _____ is a business, economics or investment term that refers to an asset's ability to be easily converted through an act of buying or selling without causing a significant movement in the price and with minimum loss of value. Money, or cash on hand, is the most liquid asset. An act of exchange of a less liquid asset with a more liquid asset is called liquidation.

   a. Spot rate
   b. Financial instruments
   c. Transfer agent
   d. Market liquidity

6. In finance, or business _____ is the ability of an entity to pay its debts with available cash. _____ can also be described as the ability of a corporation to meet its long-term fixed expenses and to accomplish long-term expansion and growth. The better a company's _____, the better it is financially.

   a. Capital asset
   b. BMC Software, Inc.
   c. Solvency
   d. 3M Company

7. In accounting, _____ is the original monetary value of an economic item. In some circumstances, assets and liabilities may be shown at their _____, as if there had been no change in value since the date of acquisition. The balance sheet value of the item may therefore differ from the 'true' value.

   a. Historical cost
   b. Bottom line
   c. Cost of goods sold
   d. Matching principle

Chapter 5. Balance Sheet and Statement of Cash Flows,

8. The _____ founded on April 1, 2001 is the successor of the International Accounting Standards Committee (IASC) founded in June 1973 in London. It is responsible for developing the International Financial Reporting Standards (new name for the International Accounting Standards issued after 2001), and promoting the use and application of these standards.

The _____ is an independent, privately-funded accounting standard-setter based in London, UK.

   a. Information Systems Audit and Control Association
   b. Institute of Management Accountants
   c. Emerging technologies
   d. International Accounting Standards Board

9. In economics, business, retail, and accounting, a _____ is the value of money that has been used up to produce something, and hence is not available for use anymore. In economics, a _____ is an alternative that is given up as a result of a decision. In business, the _____ may be one of acquisition, in which case the amount of money expended to acquire it is counted as _____.

   a. Cost of quality
   b. Prime cost
   c. Cost
   d. Cost allocation

10. _____ are formal records of a business' financial activities.

In British English, including United Kingdom company law, _____ are often referred to as accounts, although the term _____ is also used, particularly by accountants.

_____ provide an overview of a business' financial condition in both short and long term.

   a. 3M Company
   b. Notes to the financial statements
   c. Statement of retained earnings
   d. Financial statements

11. _____ is one of a series of accounting transactions dealing with the billing of customers who owe money to a person, company or organization for goods and services that have been provided to the customer. In most business entities this is typically done by generating an invoice and mailing or electronically delivering it to the customer, who in turn must pay it within an established timeframe called credit or payment terms.

An example of a common payment term is Net 30, meaning payment is due in the amount of the invoice 30 days from the date of invoice.

   a. Accrual
   b. Adjusting entries
   c. Accrued revenue
   d. Accounts receivable

12. In business and accounting, _____ are everything of value that is owned by a person or company. It is a claim on the property your income of a borrower. The balance sheet of a firm records the monetary value of the _____ owned by the firm.

   a. Earnings before interest, taxes, depreciation and amortization
   b. Accrual basis accounting
   c. Accounts receivable
   d. Assets

Chapter 5. Balance Sheet and Statement of Cash Flows,

13. _____ are the most liquid assets found within the asset portion of a company's balance sheet. Cash equivalents are assets that are readily convertible into cash, such as money market holdings, short-term government bonds or Treasury bills, marketable securities and commercial paper. _____ are distinguished from other investments through their short-term existence; they mature within 3 months whereas short-term investments are 12 months or less, and long-term investments are any investments that mature in excess of 12 months.

    a. Par value
    b. Cash and cash equivalents
    c. Debtor
    d. Payback period

14. In accounting, a _____ is an asset on the balance sheet which is expected to be sold or otherwise used up in the near future, usually within one year, or one business cycle - whichever is longer. Typical _____s include cash, cash equivalents, accounts receivable, inventory, the portion of prepaid accounts which will be used within a year, and short-term investments.

On the balance sheet, assets will typically be classified into _____s and long-term assets.

    a. Pro forma
    b. General ledger
    c. Deferred
    d. Current asset

15. _____ is a specific term used in companies' financial reporting from the company-whole point of view. Because that use excludes the effects of changing ownership interest, an economic measure of _____ is necessary for financial analysis from the shareholders' point of view

_____ is defined by the Financial Accounting Standards Board, or FASB, as 'the change in equity [net assets] of a business enterprise during a period from transactions and other events and circumstances from nonowner sources. It includes all changes in equity during a period except those resulting from investments by owners and distributions to owners.'

_____ is the sum of net income and other items that must bypass the income statement because they have not been realized, including items like an unrealized holding gain or loss from available for sale securities and foreign currency translation gains or losses.

    a. BMC Software, Inc.
    b. BNSF Railway
    c. 3M Company
    d. Comprehensive income

16. _____ are the earnings returned on the initial investment amount.

In the US, the Financial Accounting Standards Board (FASB) requires companies' income statements to report _____ for each of the major categories of the income statement: continuing operations, discontinued operations, extraordinary items, and net income.

The _____ formula does not include preferred dividends for categories outside of continued operations and net income.

a. Invested capital
b. Average accounting return
c. Earnings per share
d. Earnings yield

17. In financial accounting, a _____ is defined as an obligation of an entity arising from past transactions or events, the settlement of which may result in the transfer or use of assets, provision of services or other yielding of economic benefits in the future.
   a. False Claims Act
   b. Corporate governance
   c. Vested
   d. Liability

18. _____ refers to services paid for in advance. Examples include tolls, pay as you go cell phones, and stored-value cards such as gift cards and preloaded credit cards. _____ accounts are assets, and they are increased by debiting the account(s.)
   a. BNSF Railway
   b. BMC Software, Inc.
   c. 3M Company
   d. Prepaid

19. _____, in accrual accounting, is any account where the asset or liability is not realized until a future date (accounting period), e.g. annuities, charges, taxes, income, etc. The _____ item may be carried, dependent on type of deferral, as either an asset or liability.
   a. Pro forma
   b. Payroll
   c. Deferred
   d. Cash basis accounting

20. In economics, the concept of the _____ refers to the decision-making time frame of a firm in which at least one factor of production is fixed. Costs which are fixed in the _____ have no impact on a firms decisions. For example a firm can raise output by increasing the amount of labour through overtime.
   a. 3M Company
   b. BMC Software, Inc.
   c. Long-run
   d. Short-run

21. In accounting/accountancy, _____ are journal entries usually made at the end of an accounting period to allocate income and expenditure to the period in which they actually occurred. The revenue recognition principle is the basis of making _____ that pertain to unearned and accrued revenues under accrual-basis accounting. They are sometimes called Balance Day adjustments because they are made on balance day.
   a. Earnings before interest, taxes, depreciation and amortization
   b. Accrual
   c. Adjusting entries
   d. Accrued expense

22. In accounting, _____ has a very specific meaning. It is an outflow of cash or other valuable assets from a person or company to another person or company. This outflow of cash is generally one side of a trade for products or services that have equal or better current or future value to the buyer than to the seller.
   a. AIG
   b. Expense
   c. ABC Television Network
   d. AMEX

23. In finance, _____ is the process of estimating the potential market value of a financial asset or liability. They can be done on assets (for example, investments in marketable securities such as stocks, options, business enterprises, or intangible assets such as patents and trademarks) or on liabilities (e.g., Bonds issued by a company.) A _____ is required in many contexts including investment analysis, capital budgeting, merger and acquisition transactions, financial reporting, taxable events to determine the proper tax liability, and in litigation.

a. Disclosure
b. Vyborg Appeal
c. Daybook
d. Valuation

24. A _____ is a fungible, negotiable instrument representing financial value. they are broadly categorized into debt securities (such as banknotes, bonds and debentures), and equity securities; e.g., common stocks. The company or other entity issuing the _____ is called the issuer.
   a. BMC Software, Inc.
   b. Tracking stock
   c. 3M Company
   d. Security

25. _____ is that which is owed; usually referencing assets owed, but the term can also cover moral obligations and other interactions not requiring money. In the case of assets, _____ is a means of using future purchasing power in the present before a summation has been earned. Some companies and corporations use _____ as a part of their overall corporate finance strategy.
   a. Loan
   b. Lender
   c. Debt
   d. Debenture

26. _____ is a life of security. It may also refer to the final payment date of a loan or other financial instrument, at which point all remaining interest and principal is due to be paid.

1, 3, 6 months _____ band can be calculated by using 30-day per month periods. For _____ bands over a year it is acceptable to use 365 day per year. For example with a Treasury Bond, its _____ is the date on which the principal is paid.

   a. Maturity
   b. Factor
   c. The Goodyear Tire ' Rubber Company
   d. Statements of Financial Accounting Standards No. 133, Accounting for Derivative Instruments and Hedging Activities

27. In economic models, the _____ time frame assumes no fixed factors of production. Firms can enter or leave the marketplace, and the cost (and availability) of land, labor, raw materials, and capital goods can be assumed to vary. In contrast, in the short-run time frame, certain factors are assumed to be fixed, because there is not sufficient time for them to change.
   a. 3M Company
   b. Long-run
   c. Short-run
   d. BMC Software, Inc.

28. _____ is any physical or virtual entity that is owned by an individual or jointly by a group of individuals. An owner of _____ has the right to consume, sell, rent, mortgage, transfer and exchange his or her _____. Important widely-recognized types of _____ include real _____, personal _____ (other physical possessions), and intellectual _____ (rights over artistic creations, inventions, etc.), although the latter is not always as widely recognized or enforced.
   a. Fiduciary
   b. Property
   c. Primary authority
   d. Disclosure requirement

29. _____, also known as property, plant, and equipment (PP&E), is a term used in accountancy for assets and property which cannot easily be converted into cash. This can be compared with current assets such as cash or bank accounts, which are described as liquid assets. In most cases, only tangible assets are referred to as fixed.

a. Bankruptcy prediction
c. Minority interest
b. Fixed asset
d. Subledger

30. _____ are defined as identifiable non-monetary assets that cannot be seen, touched or physically measured, which are created through time and/or effort and that are identifiable as a separate asset. There are two primary forms of intangibles - legal intangibles (such as trade secrets (e.g., customer lists), copyrights, patents, trademarks, and goodwill) and competitive intangibles (such as knowledge activities (know-how, knowledge), collaboration activities, leverage activities, and structural activities.) Legal intangibles are known under the generic term intellectual property and generate legal property rights defensible in a court of law.
   a. ABC Television Network
   c. Overhead
   b. AIG
   d. Intangible assets

31. _____ is a financial metric which represents operating liquidity available to a business. Along with fixed assets such as plant and equipment, _____ is considered a part of operating capital. It is calculated as current assets minus current liabilities.
   a. BMC Software, Inc.
   c. Working capital management
   b. Working capital
   d. 3M Company

32. _____ are liabilities with a future benefit over one year, such as notes payable that mature greater than one year.

In accounting, the _____ are shown on the right wing of the balance-sheet representing the sources of funds, which are generally bounded in form of capital assets.

Examples of _____ are debentures, mortgage loans and other bank loans (note: not all bank loans are long term as not all are paid over a period greater than a year, the example is bridging loan.)

   a. Gross sales
   c. Cash basis accounting
   b. Book value
   d. Long-term liabilities

33. _____ are additional notes and information added to the end of the financial statements to supplement the reader with more information. Notes to Financial Statements help explain the computation of specific items in the financial statements as well as provide a more comprehensive assessment of a company's financial condition. Notes to Financial Statements can include information on debt, going concern, accounts, contingent liabilities, or contextual information explaining the financial numbers (e.g. to indicate a lawsuit.)
   a. Financial statements
   c. Notes to the financial statements
   b. Statement of retained earnings
   d. 3M Company

34. _____ were published by Accounting Principles Board (APB.) The board was created by American Institute of Certified Public Accountants (AICPA) in 1959 and was replaced by Financial Accounting Standards Board (FASB) in 1973. Its mission was to develop an overall conceptual framework of US generally accepted accounting principles (US GAAP.)
   a. AMEX
   c. AIG
   b. ABC Television Network
   d. Accounting Principles Board Opinions

35. _____ is the art of predicting bankruptcy and various measures of financial distress of public firms. It is a vast area of finance and accounting research. The importance of the area is due in part to the relevance for creditors and investors in evaluating the likelihood that a firm may go bankrupt.

Chapter 5. Balance Sheet and Statement of Cash Flows,

a. Lower of Cost or Market
b. Minority interest
c. Certified Practising Accountant
d. Bankruptcy prediction

36. _____, also called fair price (in a commonplace conflation of the two distinct concepts), is a concept used in finance and economics, defined as a rational and unbiased estimate of the potential market price of a good, service, or asset, taking into account such objective factors as:

- acquisition/production/distribution costs, replacement costs, or costs of close substitutes
- actual utility at a given level of development of social productive capability
- supply vs. demand

and subjective factors such as

- risk characteristics
- cost of capital
- individually perceived utility

In accounting, _____ is used as an estimate of the market value of an asset (or liability) for which a market price cannot be determined (usually because there is no established market for the asset.) Under GAAP (FAS 157), _____ is the amount at which the asset could be bought or sold in a current transaction between willing parties, or transferred to an equivalent party, other than in a liquidation sale. This is used for assets whose carrying value is based on mark-to-market valuations; for assets carried at historical cost, the _____ of the asset is not used. One example of where _____ is an issue is a College kitchen with a cost of $2 million which was built 5 years ago.

a. BNSF Railway
b. 3M Company
c. Fair value
d. BMC Software, Inc.

37. An _____ is a practitioner of accountancy, which is the measurement, disclosure or provision of assurance about financial information that helps managers, investors, tax authorities and other decision makers make resource allocation decisions.

The word '_____' is derived from the French 'Compter' which took its origin from the Latin 'Computare'. The word was formerly written in English as 'Accomptant', but in process of time the word, which was always pronounced by dropping the 'p', became gradually changed both in pronunciation and in orthography to its present form.

a. AMEX
b. AIG
c. ABC Television Network
d. Accountant

38. The _____ is the national, professional association of CPAs in the United States, with more than 330,000 members, including CPAs in business and industry, public practice, government, and education; student affiliates; and international associates. It sets ethical standards for the profession and U.S. auditing standards for audits of private companies; federal, state and local governments; and non-profit organizations.

Approximately 40% of its members are engaged in the practice of public accounting, in areas such as auditing, accounting, taxation, general business consulting, business valuation, personal financial planning and business technology.

a. AIG
b. ABC Television Network
c. Other postemployment benefits
d. American Institute of Certified Public Accountants

39. _____ is the statutory title of qualified accountants in the United States who have passed the Uniform _____ Examination and have met additional state education and experience requirements for certification as a _____. Individuals who have passed the Exam but have not either accomplished the required on-the-job experience or have previously met it but in the meantime have lapsed their continuing professional education are, in many states, permitted the designation '_____ Inactive' or an equivalent phrase. In most U.S. states, only _____s who are licensed are able to provide to the public attestation (including auditing) opinions on financial statements.

a. Chartered Certified Accountant
b. Chartered Accountant
c. Certified General Accountant
d. Certified Public Accountant

40. _____ means the giving out of information, either voluntarily or to be in compliance with legal regulations or workplace rules.

- In Computer security, full _____ means disclosing full information about vulnerabilities.
- In computing, _____ widget
- Journalism, full _____ refers to disclosing the interests of the writer which may bear on the subject being written about, for example, if the writer has worked with an interview subject in the past.

- In law:
    - The law of England and Wales, _____ refers to a process that may form part of legal proceedings, whereby parties inform to other parties the existence of any relevant documents that are, or have been, in their control. This compares with the process known as discovery in the course of legal proceedings in the United States.
    - In U.S. civil procedure (litigation rules for civil cases), _____ is a stage prior to trial. In civil cases, each party must disclose to the opposing party the following: names of witnesses which it may use to support its side, copies of documents (or mere description of these documents) in its control which it may use to support its side, computation of damages claimed, and certain insurance information. _____ is related to, but technically prior to, the discovery stage.
    - In Company law (known as 'corporate law' in the United States), _____ refers to giving out information about public or limited companies or their officers, which might be kept secret if the company was a private company or a partnership.

- In real property transactions, _____ refers to providing to a buyer information known to the seller or broker/agent concerning the condition or other aspects of real property that would affect the property's value or desirability. These rules regarding what information must be disclosed, and whether the information must be disclosed even if a buyer does not ask, vary from one jurisdiction to the next.

a. Trailing
b. Tax harmonisation
c. Controlled Foreign Corporations
d. Disclosure

41. _____s are cash, evidence of an ownership interest in an entity or deliver, cash or another _____.

_____s can be categorized by form depending on whether they are cash instruments or derivative instruments:

- Cash instruments are _____s whose value is determined directly by markets. They can be divided into securities, which are readily transferable, and other cash instruments such as loans and deposits, where both borrower and lender have to agree on a transfer.
- Derivative instruments are _____s which derive their value from the value and characteristics of one or more underlying assets. They can be divided into exchange-traded derivatives and over-the-counter (OTC) derivatives.

Alternatively, _____s can be categorized by 'asset class' depending on whether they are equity based (reflecting ownership of the issuing entity) or debt based (reflecting a loan the investor has made to the issuing entity.) If it is debt, it can be further categorised into short term (less than one year) or long term.

Foreign Exchange instruments and transactions are neither debt nor equity based and belong in their own category.

a. Market price
b. Financial instruments
c. Financial instrument
d. Mark-to-market

42. _____ are cash, evidence of an ownership interest in an entity, or a contractual right to receive, or deliver, cash or another financial instrument.

_____ can be categorized by form depending on whether they are cash instruments or derivative instruments:

- Cash instruments are _____ whose value is determined directly by markets. They can be divided into securities, which are readily transferable, and other cash instruments such as loans and deposits, where both borrower and lender have to agree on a transfer.
- Derivative instruments are _____ which derive their value from the value and characteristics of one or more underlying assets. They can be divided into exchange-traded derivatives and over-the-counter (OTC) derivatives.

Alternatively, _____ can be categorized by 'asset class' depending on whether they are equity based (reflecting ownership of the issuing entity) or debt based (reflecting a loan the investor has made to the issuing entity.) If it is debt, it can be further categorised into short term (less than one year) or long term.

Foreign Exchange instruments and transactions are neither debt nor equity based and belong in their own category.

Chapter 5. Balance Sheet and Statement of Cash Flows, 41

a. Transfer agent
c. Market liquidity
b. Spot rate
d. Financial instruments

43. Procter is a surname, and may also refer to:

- Bryan Waller Procter (pseud. Barry Cornwall), English poet
- Goodwin Procter, American law firm
- _____, consumer products multinational

a. Markup
c. Welfare
b. Screening
d. Procter ' Gamble

44. In financial accounting, a _____ or Statement of cash flows is a financial statement that shows a company's flow of cash. The money coming into the business is called cash inflow, and money going out from the business is called cash outflow. The statement shows how changes in balance sheet and income accounts affect cash and cash equivalents, and breaks the analysis down to operating, investing, and financing activities.
a. BNSF Railway
c. 3M Company
b. BMC Software, Inc.
d. Cash flow statement

45. _____ is the balance of the amounts of cash being received and paid by a business during a defined period of time, sometimes tied to a specific project. Measurement of _____ can be used

- to evaluate the state or performance of a business or project.
- to determine problems with liquidity. Being profitable does not necessarily mean being liquid. A company can fail because of a shortage of cash, even while profitable.
- to project rate of returns. The time of _____s into and out of projects are used as inputs to financial models such as internal rate of return, and net present value.
- to examine income or growth of a business when it is believed that accrual accounting concepts do not represent economic realities. Alternately, _____ can be used to 'validate' the net income generated by accrual accounting.

_____ as a generic term may be used differently depending on context, and certain _____ definitions may be adapted by analysts and users for their own uses. Common terms include operating _____ and free _____.

a. Controlling interest
c. Commercial paper
b. Flow-through entity
d. Cash flow

46. A _____ is a party (e.g. person, organization, company, or government) that has a claim to the services of a second party. It is a person or institution to whom money is owed. The first party, in general, has provided some property or service to the second party under the assumption (usually enforced by contract) that the second party will return an equivalent property or service.
a. Treasury company
c. Payback period
b. Par value
d. Creditor

Chapter 5. Balance Sheet and Statement of Cash Flows,

47. _____ is equal to the income that a firm has after subtracting costs and expenses from the total revenue. _____ can be distributed among holders of common stock as a dividend or held by the firm as retained earnings.

The items deducted will typically include tax expense, financing expense (interest expense), and minority interest. Likewise, preferred stock dividends will be subtracted too, though they are not an expense.

a. Generally accepted accounting principles
b. Long-term liabilities
c. Net income
d. Matching principle

48. In corporate finance, _____ is a cash flow available for distribution among all the security holders of a company. They include equity holders, debt holders, preferred stock holders, convertible security holders, and so on.

a. Procurement
b. Tax profit
c. Free cash flow
d. Product life cycle

49. _____ (NYSE: DE) is an American corporation based in Moline, Illinois, and the leading manufacturer of agricultural machinery in the world. In 2008, it was listed as 102nd in the Fortune 500 ranking. Deere and Company agricultural products, usually sold under the John Deere name, include tractors, combine harvesters, balers, planters/seeders, ATVs and forestry equipment.

a. Governmental Accounting Standards Board
b. Freddie Mac
c. Professional association
d. Deere ' Company

Chapter 6. Accounting and the Time Value of Money,

1. _____ is the value on a given date of a future payment or series of future payments, discounted to reflect the time value of money and other factors such as investment risk. _____ calculations are widely used in business and economics to provide a means to compare cash flows at different times on a meaningful 'like to like' basis.

The most commonly applied model of the time value of money is compound interest.

   a. 3M Company
   c. Future value
   b. Net present value
   d. Present value

2. _____ is the concept of adding accumulated interest back to the principal, so that interest is earned on interest from that moment on. The act of declaring interest to be principal is called compounding (i.e., interest is compounded.) A loan, for example, may have its interest compounded every month: in this case, a loan with $100 principal and 1% interest per month would have a balance of $101 at the end of the first month.

   a. Trademark
   c. Compound interest
   b. Risk management
   d. Kanban

3. A _____ is a party (e.g. person, organization, company, or government) that has a claim to the services of a second party. It is a person or institution to whom money is owed. The first party, in general, has provided some property or service to the second party under the assumption (usually enforced by contract) that the second party will return an equivalent property or service.

   a. Creditor
   c. Payback period
   b. Par value
   d. Treasury company

4. _____ means the giving out of information, either voluntarily or to be in compliance with legal regulations or workplace rules.

- In Computer security, full _____ means disclosing full information about vulnerabilities.
- In computing, _____ widget
- Journalism, full _____ refers to disclosing the interests of the writer which may bear on the subject being written about, for example, if the writer has worked with an interview subject in the past.

- In law:
    - The law of England and Wales, _____ refers to a process that may form part of legal proceedings, whereby parties inform to other parties the existence of any relevant documents that are, or have been, in their control. This compares with the process known as discovery in the course of legal proceedings in the United States.
    - In U.S. civil procedure (litigation rules for civil cases), _____ is a stage prior to trial. In civil cases, each party must disclose to the opposing party the following: names of witnesses which it may use to support its side, copies of documents (or mere description of these documents) in its control which it may use to support its side, computation of damages claimed, and certain insurance information. _____ is related to, but technically prior to, the discovery stage.
    - In Company law (known as 'corporate law' in the United States), _____ refers to giving out information about public or limited companies or their officers, which might be kept secret if the company was a private company or a partnership.

- In real property transactions, _____ refers to providing to a buyer information known to the seller or broker/agent concerning the condition or other aspects of real property that would affect the property's value or desirability. These rules regarding what information must be disclosed, and whether the information must be disclosed even if a buyer does not ask, vary from one jurisdiction to the next.

a. Controlled Foreign Corporations
b. Tax harmonisation
c. Trailing
d. Disclosure

5. _____, also called fair price (in a commonplace conflation of the two distinct concepts), is a concept used in finance and economics, defined as a rational and unbiased estimate of the potential market price of a good, service, or asset, taking into account such objective factors as:

- acquisition/production/distribution costs, replacement costs, or costs of close substitutes
- actual utility at a given level of development of social productive capability
- supply vs. demand

and subjective factors such as

- risk characteristics
- cost of capital
- individually perceived utility

Chapter 6. Accounting and the Time Value of Money,

In accounting, _____ is used as an estimate of the market value of an asset (or liability) for which a market price cannot be determined (usually because there is no established market for the asset.) Under GAAP (FAS 157), _____ is the amount at which the asset could be bought or sold in a current transaction between willing parties, or transferred to an equivalent party, other than in a liquidation sale. This is used for assets whose carrying value is based on mark-to-market valuations; for assets carried at historical cost, the _____ of the asset is not used. One example of where _____ is an issue is a College kitchen with a cost of $2 million which was built 5 years ago.

- a. BNSF Railway
- b. Fair Value
- c. 3M Company
- d. BMC Software, Inc.

6. _____s are cash, evidence of an ownership interest in an entity or deliver, cash or another _____.

_____s can be categorized by form depending on whether they are cash instruments or derivative instruments:

- Cash instruments are _____s whose value is determined directly by markets. They can be divided into securities, which are readily transferable, and other cash instruments such as loans and deposits, where both borrower and lender have to agree on a transfer.
- Derivative instruments are _____s which derive their value from the value and characteristics of one or more underlying assets. They can be divided into exchange-traded derivatives and over-the-counter (OTC) derivatives.

Alternatively, _____s can be categorized by 'asset class' depending on whether they are equity based (reflecting ownership of the issuing entity) or debt based (reflecting a loan the investor has made to the issuing entity.) If it is debt, it can be further categorised into short term (less than one year) or long term.

Foreign Exchange instruments and transactions are neither debt nor equity based and belong in their own category.

- a. Financial instruments
- b. Market price
- c. Mark-to-market
- d. Financial Instrument

7. _____ are cash, evidence of an ownership interest in an entity, or a contractual right to receive, or deliver, cash or another financial instrument.

_____ can be categorized by form depending on whether they are cash instruments or derivative instruments:

- Cash instruments are _____ whose value is determined directly by markets. They can be divided into securities, which are readily transferable, and other cash instruments such as loans and deposits, where both borrower and lender have to agree on a transfer.
- Derivative instruments are _____ which derive their value from the value and characteristics of one or more underlying assets. They can be divided into exchange-traded derivatives and over-the-counter (OTC) derivatives.

Alternatively, _____ can be categorized by 'asset class' depending on whether they are equity based (reflecting ownership of the issuing entity) or debt based (reflecting a loan the investor has made to the issuing entity.) If it is debt, it can be further categorised into short term (less than one year) or long term.

Foreign Exchange instruments and transactions are neither debt nor equity based and belong in their own category.

- a. Transfer agent
- b. Financial Instruments
- c. Market liquidity
- d. Spot rate

8. A _____ is a type of debt Like all debt instruments, a _____ entails the redistribution of financial assets over time, between the lender and the borrower.
- a. Loan
- b. Loan to value
- c. Debenture
- d. Lender

9. In economic models, the _____ time frame assumes no fixed factors of production. Firms can enter or leave the marketplace, and the cost (and availability) of land, labor, raw materials, and capital goods can be assumed to vary. In contrast, in the short-run time frame, certain factors are assumed to be fixed, because there is not sufficient time for them to change.
- a. Short-run
- b. BMC Software, Inc.
- c. 3M Company
- d. Long-run

10. The term _____ or superannuation refers to a pension granted upon retirement. They may be set up by employers, insurance companies, the government or other institutions such as employer associations or trade unions.
- a. Wage
- b. 3M Company
- c. BMC Software, Inc.
- d. Retirement plan

11. A _____ is a fund established by a government agency or business for the purpose of reducing debt.

The _____ was first used in Great Britain in the 18th century to reduce national debt. While used by Robert Walpole in 1716 and effectively in the 1720s and early 1730s, it originated in the commercial tax syndicates of the Italian peninsula of the 14th century to retire redeemable public debt of those cities.

Chapter 6. Accounting and the Time Value of Money, 47

a. Treasury company
c. Payback period

b. Segregated portfolio company
d. Sinking fund

12. In business and accounting, _____ are everything of value that is owned by a person or company. It is a claim on the property your income of a borrower. The balance sheet of a firm records the monetary value of the _____ owned by the firm.

a. Accrual basis accounting
c. Earnings before interest, taxes, depreciation and amortization

b. Assets
d. Accounts receivable

13. _____ is a fee paid on borrowed assets. It is the price paid for the use of borrowed money , or, money earned by deposited funds .Assets that are sometimes lent with _____ include money, shares, consumer goods through hire purchase, major assets such as aircraft, and even entire factories in finance lease arrangements. The _____ is calculated upon the value of the assets in the same manner as upon money.

a. Insolvency
c. AIG

b. Interest
d. ABC Television Network

14. An _____ is the price a borrower pays for the use of money they do not own, for instance a small company might borrow from a bank to kick start their business, and the return a lender receives for deferring the use of funds, by lending it to the borrower. _____s are normally expressed as a percentage rate over the period of one year.

_____s targets are also a vital tool of monetary policy and are used to control variables like investment, inflation, and unemployment.

a. ABC Television Network
c. Interest rate

b. AIG
d. AMEX

15. _____ is interest calculated only on the principal amount, or on that portion of the principal amount which remains unpaid.

The amount of _____ is calculated according to the following formula:

$$I_{simp} = (r \cdot B_0) \cdot m$$

where r is the period interest rate , B_0 the initial balance and m the number of time periods elapsed.

a. BMC Software, Inc.
c. Line of credit

b. 3M Company
d. Simple interest

16. Most patent law systems require that a patent application disclose a claimed invention in sufficient detail for the notional person skilled in the art to carry out that claimed invention. This requirement is often known as sufficiency of disclosure or enablement, depending on the jurisdiction.

Chapter 6. Accounting and the Time Value of Money,

The _____ lies at the heart and origin of patent law. A state or government grants an inventor, or the inventor's assignee, a monopoly for a given period of time in exchange for the inventor disclosing to the public how to make or practice his or her invention. If a patent fails to contain such information, then the bargain is violated, and the patent is unenforceable.

a. False Claims Act
c. Disclosure requirement

b. Tax patent
d. Pre-emption right

17. _____ measures the nominal future sum of money that a given sum of money is 'worth' at a specified time in the future assuming a certain interest rate rate of return; it is the present value multiplied by the accumulation function.

The value does not include corrections for inflation or other factors that affect the true value of money in the future. This is used in time value of money calculations.

a. Future value
c. Present value

b. 3M Company
d. Net present value

18. A _____ is a fungible, negotiable instrument representing financial value. they are broadly categorized into debt securities (such as banknotes, bonds and debentures), and equity securities; e.g., common stocks. The company or other entity issuing the _____ is called the issuer.

a. 3M Company
c. BMC Software, Inc.

b. Tracking stock
d. Security

19. _____ in the United States currently refers to the federal Old-Age, Survivors, and Disability Insurance (OASDI) program.

The original _____ Act and the current version of the Act, as amended encompass several social welfare and social insurance programs. The larger and better known programs are:

- Federal Old-Age, Survivors, and Disability Insurance
- Unemployment benefits
- Temporary Assistance for Needy Families
- Health Insurance for Aged and Disabled (Medicare)
- Grants to States for Medical Assistance Programs (Medicaid)
- State Children's Health Insurance Program (SCHIP)
- Supplemental Security Income (Social Securityl)

U.S. _____ is a social insurance program funded through dedicated payroll taxes called Federal Insurance Contributions Act (FICA.) Tax deposits are formally entrusted to Federal Old-Age and Survivors Insurance Trust Fund, or Federal Disability Insurance Trust Fund, Federal Hospital Insurance Trust Fund or the Federal Supplementary Medical Insurance Trust Fund.

Chapter 6. Accounting and the Time Value of Money,

a. Sale
b. Comparable
c. Social Security
d. Price-to-sales ratio

20. The term _____ is used in finance theory to refer to any terminating stream of fixed payments over a specified period of time. This usage is most commonly seen in academic discussions of finance, usually in connection with the valuation of the stream of payments, taking into account time value of money concepts such as interest rate and future value.

Examples of these are regular deposits to a savings account, monthly home mortgage payments and monthly insurance payments.

a. Intangible
b. Improvement
c. Appropriation
d. Annuity

21. _____ that may or may not be incurred by an entity depending on the outcome of a future event such as a court case. These liabilities are recorded in a company's accounts and shown in the balance sheet when both probable and reasonably estimable. A footnote to the balance sheet describes the nature and extent of the _____.
a. Contingent liabilities
b. Headnote
c. Nonacquiescence
d. Tangible

22. In financial accounting, a _____ is defined as an obligation of an entity arising from past transactions or events, the settlement of which may result in the transfer or use of assets, provision of services or other yielding of economic benefits in the future.
a. Liability
b. False Claims Act
c. Vested
d. Corporate governance

23. _____ is a financial mechanism in which a debtor obtains the right to delay payments to a creditor, for a defined period of time, in exchange for a charge or fee. Essentially, the party that owes money in the present purchases the right to delay the payment until some future date. The discount, or charge, is simply the difference between the original amount owed in the present and the amount that has to be paid in the future to settle the debt.
a. Risk aversion
b. Discount factor
c. Risk adjusted return on capital
d. Discounting

24. _____ is a structured finance process, which involves pooling and repackaging of cash flow producing financial assets into securities that are then sold to investors. The name '_____' is derived from the fact that the form of financial instruments used to obtain funds from the investors are securities.

As a portfolio risk backed by amortizing cash flows - and unlike general corporate debt - the credit quality of securitized debt is non-stationary due to changes in volatility that are time- and structure-dependent.

a. Cross-border leasing
b. Debtor
c. Market value
d. Securitization

25. _____, in accrual accounting, is any account where the asset or liability is not realized until a future date (accounting period), e.g. annuities, charges, taxes, income, etc. The _____ item may be carried, dependent on type of deferral, as either an asset or liability.

a. Pro forma
c. Deferred
b. Payroll
d. Cash basis accounting

26. In finance, a _____ is a debt security, in which the authorized issuer owes the holders a debt and, depending on the terms of the _____, is obliged to pay interest (the coupon) and/or to repay the principal at a later date, termed maturity. It is a formal contract to repay borrowed money with interest at fixed intervals.

Thus a _____ is like a loan: the issuer is the borrower, the _____ holder is the lender, and the coupon is the interest.

a. Zero-coupon bond
c. Revenue bonds
b. Coupon rate
d. Bond

27. In finance, _____ is the process of estimating the potential market value of a financial asset or liability. They can be done on assets (for example, investments in marketable securities such as stocks, options, business enterprises, or intangible assets such as patents and trademarks) or on liabilities (e.g., Bonds issued by a company.) A _____ is required in many contexts including investment analysis, capital budgeting, merger and acquisition transactions, financial reporting, taxable events to determine the proper tax liability, and in litigation.

a. Daybook
c. Valuation
b. Disclosure
d. Vyborg Appeal

28. _____ is the process of increasing, or accounting for, an amount over a period of time. Particular instances of the term include:

- _____, the allocation of a lump sum amount to different time periods, particularly for loans and other forms of finance, including related interest or other finance charges.
    - _____ schedule, a table detailing each periodic payment on a loan (typically a mortgage), as generated by an _____ calculator.
    - Negative _____, an _____ schedule where the loan amount actually increases through not paying the full interest
- Amortized analysis, analyzing the execution cost of algorithms over a sequence of operations.
- _____ of capital expenditures of certain assets under accounting rules, particularly intangible assets, in a manner analogous to depreciation.
- _____

a. Annuity
c. EBIT
b. Intangible
d. Amortization

Chapter 6. Accounting and the Time Value of Money, 51

29. _____ is the balance of the amounts of cash being received and paid by a business during a defined period of time, sometimes tied to a specific project. Measurement of _____ can be used

- to evaluate the state or performance of a business or project.
- to determine problems with liquidity. Being profitable does not necessarily mean being liquid. A company can fail because of a shortage of cash, even while profitable.
- to project rate of returns. The time of _____s into and out of projects are used as inputs to financial models such as internal rate of return, and net present value.
- to examine income or growth of a business when it is believed that accrual accounting concepts do not represent economic realities. Alternately, _____ can be used to 'validate' the net income generated by accrual accounting.

_____ as a generic term may be used differently depending on context, and certain _____ definitions may be adapted by analysts and users for their own uses. Common terms include operating _____ and free _____.

 a. Cash Flow
 b. Controlling interest
 c. Flow-through entity
 d. Commercial paper

30. _____ is the risk of loss due to a debtor's non-payment of a loan or other line of credit (either the principal or interest (coupon) or both)

Most lenders employ their own models (credit scorecards) to rank potential and existing customers according to risk, and then apply appropriate strategies. With products such as unsecured personal loans or mortgages, lenders charge a higher price for higher risk customers and vice versa. With revolving products such as credit cards and overdrafts, risk is controlled through the setting of credit limits.

 a. Market risk
 b. Currency risk
 c. 3M Company
 d. Credit risk

31. _____ is an acronym for First In, First Out, an abstraction in ways of organizing and manipulation of data relative to time and prioritization. This expression describes the principle of a queue processing technique or servicing conflicting demands by ordering process by first-come, first-served (FCFS) behaviour: what comes in first is handled first, what comes in next waits until the first is finished, etc.

Thus it is analogous to the behaviour of persons queueing (or 'standing in line', in common American parlance), where the persons leave the queue in the order they arrive, or waiting one's turn at a traffic control signal.

 a. Risk management
 b. Trademark
 c. Kanban
 d. FIFO

32. In economics, _____ is a rise in the general level of prices of goods and services in an economy over a period of time. When the general price level rises, each unit of currency buys fewer goods and services; consequently, _____ is also a decline in the real value of money--a loss of purchasing power in the medium of exchange which is also the monetary unit of account in the economy. A chief measure of general price-level _____ is the general _____ rate, which is the percentage change in a general price index (normally the Consumer Price Index) over time.

Chapter 6. Accounting and the Time Value of Money,

    a. Opportunity cost
    b. ABC Television Network
    c. AIG
    d. Inflation

33. _____ is a concept that denotes the precise probability of specific eventualities. Technically, the notion of _____ is independent from the notion of value and, as such, eventualities may have both beneficial and adverse consequences. However, in general usage the convention is to focus only on potential negative impact to some characteristic of value that may arise from a future event.
    a. Risk adjusted return on capital
    b. Discounting
    c. Risk
    d. Discount factor

34. A _____ is the transfer of an interest in property (or the equivalent in law - a charge) to a lender as a security for a debt - usually a loan of money. While a _____ in itself is not a debt, it is the lender's security for a debt. It is a transfer of an interest in land (or the equivalent) from the owner to the _____ lender, on the condition that this interest will be returned to the owner when the terms of the _____ have been satisfied or performed.
    a. BNSF Railway
    b. BMC Software, Inc.
    c. Mortgage
    d. 3M Company

35. An _____ is a retirement plan account that provides some tax advantages for retirement savings in the United States.

The _____ and related vehicles were created by amendments to the Internal Revenue Code of 1954 (as amended) made by the Employee Retirement Income Security Act of 1974 (ERISA), which enacted (among other things) Internal Revenue Code sections 219 (26 U.S.C. § 219) and 408 (26 U.S.C.

    a. Implied level of government service
    b. Equity of condition
    c. Indirect tax
    d. Individual Retirement Arrangement

36. Procter is a surname, and may also refer to:

- Bryan Waller Procter (pseud. Barry Cornwall), English poet
- Goodwin Procter, American law firm
- _____, consumer products multinational

    a. Welfare
    b. Screening
    c. Markup
    d. Procter ' Gamble

Chapter 7. Cash and Receivables, 53

1. _____ are the most liquid assets found within the asset portion of a company's balance sheet. Cash equivalents are assets that are readily convertible into cash, such as money market holdings, short-term government bonds or Treasury bills, marketable securities and commercial paper. _____ are distinguished from other investments through their short-term existence; they mature within 3 months whereas short-term investments are 12 months or less, and long-term investments are any investments that mature in excess of 12 months.

   a. Par value
   b. Payback period
   c. Debtor
   d. Cash and cash equivalents

2. _____ is the balance of the amounts of cash being received and paid by a business during a defined period of time, sometimes tied to a specific project. Measurement of _____ can be used

   - to evaluate the state or performance of a business or project.
   - to determine problems with liquidity. Being profitable does not necessarily mean being liquid. A company can fail because of a shortage of cash, even while profitable.
   - to project rate of returns. The time of _____s into and out of projects are used as inputs to financial models such as internal rate of return, and net present value.
   - to examine income or growth of a business when it is believed that accrual accounting concepts do not represent economic realities. Alternately, _____ can be used to 'validate' the net income generated by accrual accounting.

   _____ as a generic term may be used differently depending on context, and certain _____ definitions may be adapted by analysts and users for their own uses. Common terms include operating _____ and free _____.

   a. Cash flow
   b. Commercial paper
   c. Controlling interest
   d. Flow-through entity

3. In financial accounting, a _____ or Statement of cash flows is a financial statement that shows a company's flow of cash. The money coming into the business is called cash inflow, and money going out from the business is called cash outflow. The statement shows how changes in balance sheet and income accounts affect cash and cash equivalents, and breaks the analysis down to operating, investing, and financing activities.

   a. Cash flow statement
   b. BNSF Railway
   c. 3M Company
   d. BMC Software, Inc.

4. A _____ is a time deposit, a financial product commonly offered to consumers by banks, thrift institutions, and credit unions.

   They are similar to savings accounts in that they are insured and thus virtually risk-free; they are 'money in the bank' (_____s are insured by the FDIC for banks or by the NCUA for credit unions.) They are different from savings accounts in that the _____ has a specific, fixed term (often three months, six months, or one to five years), and, usually, a fixed interest rate.

   a. Reserve requirement
   b. Prime rate
   c. Transactional account
   d. Certificate of deposit

Chapter 7. Cash and Receivables,

5. In the global money market, _____ is an unsecured promissory note with a fixed maturity of one to 270 days. _____ is a money-market security issued (sold) by large banks and corporations to get money to meet short term debt obligations (for example, payroll), and is only backed by an issuing bank or corporation's promise to pay the face amount on the maturity date specified on the note. Since it is not backed by collateral, only firms with excellent credit ratings from a recognized rating agency will be able to sell their _____ at a reasonable price.
   a. Controlling interest
   b. Commercial paper
   c. Flow-through entity
   d. Gross profit margin

6. _____, commonly known as e-commerce or eCommerce, consists of the buying and selling of products or services over electronic systems such as the Internet and other computer networks. The amount of trade conducted electronically has grown extraordinarily since the spread of the Internet. A wide variety of commerce is conducted in this way, spurring and drawing on innovations in electronic funds transfer, supply chain management, Internet marketing, online transaction processing, electronic data interchange (EDI), inventory management systems, and automated data collection systems.
   a. AIG
   b. Electronic data interchange
   c. Electronic commerce
   d. ABC Television Network

7. In finance, the _____ is the global financial market for short-term borrowing and lending. It provides short-term liquidity funding for the global financial system. The _____ is where short-term obligations such as Treasury bills, commercial paper and bankers' acceptances are bought and sold.
   a. Money market
   b. Restructuring
   c. Securitization
   d. Segregated portfolio company

8. _____ is often a small amount of discretionary funds in the form of cash used for expenditures where it is not sensible to make the disbursement by check, because of the inconvenience and costs of writing, signing and then cashing the check.

The most common way of accounting expenditures is to use the imprest system. The initial fund would be created by issuing a check for the desired amount.

   a. Minority interest
   b. Petty cash
   c. Remittance advice
   d. Fixed asset

9. In banking, _____ refers to checks which have been written by the maker for a date in the future _____ checks are often used in conjunction with payday loans.
   a. BMC Software, Inc.
   b. 3M Company
   c. BNSF Railway
   d. Postdated

10. In economics, the concept of the _____ refers to the decision-making time frame of a firm in which at least one factor of production is fixed. Costs which are fixed in the _____ have no impact on a firms decisions. For example a firm can raise output by increasing the amount of labour through overtime.
    a. Long-run
    b. BMC Software, Inc.
    c. 3M Company
    d. Short-run

Chapter 7. Cash and Receivables,

11. Treasury securities are government debt issued by the United States Department of the Treasury through the Bureau of the Public Debt. They are the debt financing instruments of the U.S. Federal government, and they are often referred to simply as Treasuries or Treasurys. There are four types of marketable treasury securities: _____, Treasury notes, Treasury bonds, and Treasury Inflation Protected Securities (TIPS.)

_____ mature in one year or less. Like zero-coupon bonds, they do not pay interest prior to maturity; instead they are sold at a discount of the par value to create a positive yield to maturity. Many regard _____ as the least risky investment available to U.S. investors.

    a. BMC Software, Inc.
    c. 3M Company
    b. Treasury bills
    d. BNSF Railway

12. An _____ is a term used in behavioral economics to describe those types of behaviors that impose costs on a person in the long-run that are not taken into account when making decisions in the present. Classical Economics discourages government from creating legislation that targets internalities, because it is assumed that the consumer takes these personal costs into account when paying for the good that causes the _____. For example, cigarettes should be taxed because of the negative consumption externalities that they impose, such as second-hand smoke, not because the smoker harms him or herself by smoking.

    a. Authorised capital
    c. Inventory turnover ratio
    b. Operating budget
    d. Internality

13. In accounting and organizational theory, _____ is defined as a process effected by an organization's structure, work and authority flows, people and management information systems, designed to help the organization accomplish specific goals or objectives. It is a means by which an organization's resources are directed, monitored, and measured. It plays an important role in preventing and detecting fraud and protecting the organization's resources, both physical (e.g., machinery and property) and intangible (e.g., reputation or intellectual property such as trademarks.)

    a. Audit committee
    c. Auditor independence
    b. Audit risk
    d. Internal control

14. A _____ is the transfer of wealth from one party (such as a person or company) to another. A _____ is usually made in exchange for the provision of goods, services or both, or to fulfill a legal obligation.

The simplest and oldest form of _____ is barter, the exchange of one good or service for another.

    a. 3M Company
    c. Payee
    b. BMC Software, Inc.
    d. Payment

15. _____ is a business, economics or investment term that refers to an asset's ability to be easily converted through an act of buying or selling without causing a significant movement in the price and with minimum loss of value. Money, or cash on hand, is the most liquid asset. An act of exchange of a less liquid asset with a more liquid asset is called liquidation.

    a. Transfer agent
    c. Financial instruments
    b. Spot rate
    d. Market liquidity

16. A _____ is a fungible, negotiable instrument representing financial value. they are broadly categorized into debt securities (such as banknotes, bonds and debentures), and equity securities; e.g., common stocks. The company or other entity issuing the _____ is called the issuer.

Chapter 7. Cash and Receivables,

a. Tracking stock
b. Security
c. 3M Company
d. BMC Software, Inc.

17. The U.S. _____ is an independent agency of the United States government which holds primary responsibility for enforcing the federal securities laws and regulating the securities industry, the nation's stock and options exchanges, and other electronic securities markets. The SEC was created by section 4 of the Securities Exchange Act of 1934 (now codified as 15 U.S.C. ÂÂ§ 78d and commonly referred to as the 1934 Act.)
   a. BMC Software, Inc.
   b. 3M Company
   c. BNSF Railway
   d. Securities and Exchange Commission

18. In business and accounting, _____ are everything of value that is owned by a person or company. It is a claim on the property your income of a borrower. The balance sheet of a firm records the monetary value of the _____ owned by the firm.
   a. Accounts receivable
   b. Assets
   c. Accrual basis accounting
   d. Earnings before interest, taxes, depreciation and amortization

19. In economic models, the _____ time frame assumes no fixed factors of production. Firms can enter or leave the marketplace, and the cost (and availability) of land, labor, raw materials, and capital goods can be assumed to vary. In contrast, in the short-run time frame, certain factors are assumed to be fixed, because there is not sufficient time for them to change.
   a. BMC Software, Inc.
   b. 3M Company
   c. Short-run
   d. Long-run

20. _____ are securities that can be easily converted into cash. Such securities will generally have highly liquid markets allowing the security to be sold at a reasonable price very quickly. This is a usual feature in real estate.
   a. 3M Company
   b. Tracking stock
   c. BMC Software, Inc.
   d. Marketable

21. _____ is one of a series of accounting transactions dealing with the billing of customers who owe money to a person, company or organization for goods and services that have been provided to the customer. In most business entities this is typically done by generating an invoice and mailing or electronically delivering it to the customer, who in turn must pay it within an established timeframe called credit or payment terms.

An example of a common payment term is Net 30, meaning payment is due in the amount of the invoice 30 days from the date of invoice.

   a. Adjusting entries
   b. Accounts receivable
   c. Accrued revenue
   d. Accrual

22. _____ represents claims for which formal instruments of credit are issued as evidence of debt, such as a promissory note. The credit instrument normally requires the debtor to pay interest and extends for time periods of 60-90 days or longer.
   a. Notes receivable
   b. Restricted stock
   c. Moving average
   d. Public offering

Chapter 7. Cash and Receivables,

23. A _____, also referred to as a note payable in accounting, is a contract where one party (the maker or issuer) makes an unconditional promise in writing to pay a sum of money to the other (the payee), either at a fixed or determinable future time or on demand of the payee, under specific terms. They differ from IOUs in that they contain a specific promise to pay, rather than simply acknowledging that a debt exists.

The terms of a note typically include the principal amount, the interest rate if any, and the maturity date.

   a. BNSF Railway
   c. 3M Company
   b. Promissory note
   d. BMC Software, Inc.

24. _____ are reductions to a basic price of goods or services. They can occur anywhere in the distribution channel, modifying either the manufacturer's list price (determined by the manufacturer and often printed on the package), the retail price (set by the retailer and often attached to the product with a sticker), or the list price (which is quoted to a potential buyer, usually in written form.) The market price (also called effective price) is the amount actually paid.
   a. Pricing
   c. Target costing
   b. Resale price maintenance
   d. Discounts and allowances

25. Discounting is a financial mechanism in which a debtor obtains the right to delay payments to a creditor, for a defined period of time, in exchange for a charge or fee. Essentially, the party that owes money in the present purchases the right to delay the payment until some future date. The _____, or charge, is simply the difference between the original amount owed in the present and the amount that has to be paid in the future to settle the debt.
   a. Risk aversion
   c. Discount factor
   b. Discounting
   d. Discount

26. A _____ is the pinnacle activity involved in selling products or services in return for money or other compensation. It is an act of completion of a commercial activity.

A _____ is completed by the seller, the owner of the goods.

   a. High yield stock
   c. Maturity
   b. Tertiary sector of economy
   d. Sale

27. _____ in economics and business is the result of an exchange and from that trade we assign a numerical monetary value to a good, service or asset. If Alice trades Bob 4 apples for an orange, the _____ of an orange is 4 apples. Inversely, the _____ of an apple is 1/4 oranges.
   a. Price discrimination
   c. Transactional Net Margin Method
   b. Discounts and allowances
   d. Price

28. _____ were published by Accounting Principles Board (APB.) The board was created by American Institute of Certified Public Accountants (AICPA) in 1959 and was replaced by Financial Accounting Standards Board (FASB) in 1973. Its mission was to develop an overall conceptual framework of US generally accepted accounting principles (US GAAP.)
   a. ABC Television Network
   c. AIG
   b. Accounting Principles Board Opinions
   d. AMEX

29. _____ is a fee paid on borrowed assets. It is the price paid for the use of borrowed money , or, money earned by deposited funds .Assets that are sometimes lent with _____ include money, shares, consumer goods through hire purchase, major assets such as aircraft, and even entire factories in finance lease arrangements. The _____ is calculated upon the value of the assets in the same manner as upon money.
   a. ABC Television Network
   b. AIG
   c. Insolvency
   d. Interest

30. In finance, _____ is the process of estimating the potential market value of a financial asset or liability. They can be done on assets (for example, investments in marketable securities such as stocks, options, business enterprises, or intangible assets such as patents and trademarks) or on liabilities (e.g., Bonds issued by a company.) A _____ is required in many contexts including investment analysis, capital budgeting, merger and acquisition transactions, financial reporting, taxable events to determine the proper tax liability, and in litigation.
   a. Valuation
   b. Vyborg Appeal
   c. Disclosure
   d. Daybook

31. In financial accounting and finance, _____ is the portion of receivables that can no longer be collected, typically from accounts receivable or loans. _____ in accounting is considered an expense.

There are two methods to account for _____:

1. Direct write off method (Non - GAAP)

A receivable which is not considered collectible is charged directly to the income statement.

1. Allowance method (GAAP)

An estimate is made at the end of each fiscal year of the amount of _____. This is then accumulated in a provision which is then used to reduce specific receivable accounts as and when necessary.

   a. Bad debt
   b. Total Expense Ratio
   c. 3M Company
   d. Tax expense

32. The term _____ describes a reduction in recognized value. In accounting terminology, it refers to recognition of the reduced or zero value of an asset. In income tax statements, it refers to a reduction of taxable income as recognition of certain expenses required to produce the income.
   a. Salvage value
   b. Current asset
   c. Payroll
   d. Write-off

33. In financial accounting, a _____ or statement of financial position is a summary of a person's or organization's balances. Assets, liabilities and ownership equity are listed as of a specific date, such as the end of its financial year. A _____ is often described as a snapshot of a company's financial condition.
   a. 3M Company
   b. Balance sheet
   c. Financial statements
   d. Statement of retained earnings

Chapter 7. Cash and Receivables, 59

34. The _____ is a private, not-for-profit organization whose primary purpose is to develop generally accepted accounting principles (GAAP) within the United States in the public's interest. The Securities and Exchange Commission (SEC) designated the _____ as the organization responsible for setting accounting standards for public companies in the U.S. It was created in 1973, replacing the Accounting Principles Board and the Committee on Accounting Procedure of the American Institute of Certified Public Accountants. The _____'s mission is 'to establish and improve standards of financial accounting and reporting for the guidance and education of the public, including issuers, auditors, and users of financial information.'

The _____ is not a governmental body.

  a. Public company
  c. Governmental Accounting Standards Board
  b. Fannie Mae
  d. Financial Accounting Standards Board

35. _____ is a company's financial statement that indicates how the revenue is transformed into the net income The purpose of the _____ is to show managers and investors whether the company made or lost money during the period being reported.

The important thing to remember about an _____ is that it represents a period of time.

  a. AIG
  c. ABC Television Network
  b. Income statement
  d. AMEX

36. In law, the payer is the party making a payment while the _____ is the party receiving the payment.

There are two types of payment methods; exchanging and provisioning. Exchanging is to change coin, money and banknote in terms of the price.

  a. 3M Company
  c. BMC Software, Inc.
  b. Payee
  d. Payment

37. A _____ is any one of a variety of different systems, institutions, procedures, social relations and infrastructures whereby persons trade, and goods and services are exchanged, forming part of the economy. It is an arrangement that allows buyers and sellers to exchange things. _____s vary in size, range, geographic scale, location, types and variety of human communities, as well as the types of goods and services traded.

  a. Market
  c. Market Failure
  b. Perfect competition
  d. Recession

38. _____ is the value of a coin, stamp or paper money, as printed on the coin, stamp or bill itself by the minting authority. While the _____ usually refers to the true value of the coin, stamp or bill in question (as with circulation coins) it can sometimes be largely symbolic, as is often the case with bullion coins. For example, a one troy ounce (31 g) American Gold Eagle bullion coin was worth and sold for about $670 USD during 2006 market prices (as of July 17, 2006) and yet has a _____ of only $50 USD.

  a. BMC Software, Inc.
  c. 3M Company
  b. BNSF Railway
  d. Face value

39. An _____ is the price a borrower pays for the use of money they do not own, for instance a small company might borrow from a bank to kick start their business, and the return a lender receives for deferring the use of funds, by lending it to the borrower. _____s are normally expressed as a percentage rate over the period of one year.

_____s targets are also a vital tool of monetary policy and are used to control variables like investment, inflation, and unemployment.

a. AIG
b. ABC Television Network
c. AMEX
d. Interest rate

40. In finance, the term _____ describes the amount in cash that returns to the owners of a security. Normally it does not include the price variations, at the difference of the total return. _____ applies to various stated rates of return on stocks (common and preferred, and convertible), fixed income instruments (bonds, notes, bills, strips, zero coupon), and some other investment type insurance products (e.g. annuities.)

a. Residence trusts
b. Disclosure
c. Pension System
d. Yield

41. _____ is any physical or virtual entity that is owned by an individual or jointly by a group of individuals. An owner of _____ has the right to consume, sell, rent, mortgage, transfer and exchange his or her _____. Important widely-recognized types of _____ include real _____, personal _____ (other physical possessions), and intellectual _____ (rights over artistic creations, inventions, etc.), although the latter is not always as widely recognized or enforced.

a. Property
b. Disclosure requirement
c. Primary authority
d. Fiduciary

42. _____ is a file or account that contains money that a person or company owes to suppliers, but has not paid yet (a form of debt.) When you receive an invoice you add it to the file, and then you remove it when you pay. Thus, the A/P is a form of credit that suppliers offer to their purchasers by allowing them to pay for a product or service after it has already been received.

a. Earnings before interest, taxes, depreciation and amortization
b. Accounts receivable
c. Accrual
d. Accounts payable

43. A _____ is a reduction in the general availability of loans or a sudden tightening of the conditions required to obtain a loan from the banks. A _____ generally involves a reduction in the availability of credit independent of a rise in official interest rates. In such situations, the relationship between credit availability and interest rates has implicitly changed, such that either credit becomes less available at any given official interest rate, or there ceases to be a clear relationship between interest rates and credit availability

a. Debenture
b. Debt
c. Loan
d. Credit crunch

44. _____ (NYSE: DE) is an American corporation based in Moline, Illinois, and the leading manufacturer of agricultural machinery in the world. In 2008, it was listed as 102nd in the Fortune 500 ranking. Deere and Company agricultural products, usually sold under the John Deere name, include tractors, combine harvesters, balers, planters/seeders, ATVs and forestry equipment.

Chapter 7. Cash and Receivables, 61

    a. Governmental Accounting Standards Board   b. Freddie Mac
    c. Professional association   d. Deere ' Company

45. A _____ is a habit, a preparation, a state of readiness, or a tendency to act in a specified way.

The terms dispositional belief and occurrent belief refer, in the former case, to a belief that is held in the mind but not currently being considered, and in the latter case, to a belief that is currently being considered by the mind.

In Bourdieu's theory of fields _____s are the natural tendencies of each individual to take on a certain position in any field.

    a. BMC Software, Inc.   b. Disposition
    c. BNSF Railway   d. 3M Company

46. In mathematics _____s are numbers or other things that get multiplied. In particular, see:

- Factorization, the decomposition of an object into a product of other objects
- Integer factorization, the process of breaking down a composite number into smaller non-trivial divisors
- A coefficient
- A divisor of a particular number, or of an element of a monoid
- A von Neumann algebra with a trivial center

In statistics

- _____ analysis is the study of how _____s or certain variables affect variables.

In technology:

- Human _____s, a profession that focuses on how people interact with products, tools, or procedures
- 'Functionality, Application domain, Conditions, Technology, Objects and Responsibility;', In object-oriented programming

In computer science and information technology:

- Authentication _____, a piece of information used to verify a person's identity for security purposes
- _____, a Unix command for numbers factorization
- _____ (programming language), an experimental Forth-like programming language

In television:

- The O'Reilly _____, an American talk show hosted by Bill O'Reilly on Fox News.
- The Krypton _____, a British game show hosted by Gordon Burns, formally on ITV. Also had an American version.

Chapter 7. Cash and Receivables,

a. Valuation
c. Factor
b. The Goodyear Tire ' Rubber Company
d. Merck ' Co., Inc.

47. In financial accounting, a _____ is defined as an obligation of an entity arising from past transactions or events, the settlement of which may result in the transfer or use of assets, provision of services or other yielding of economic benefits in the future.

a. Vested
c. Corporate governance
b. False Claims Act
d. Liability

48. _____ is a structured finance process, which involves pooling and repackaging of cash flow producing financial assets into securities that are then sold to investors. The name '_____' is derived from the fact that the form of financial instruments used to obtain funds from the investors are securities.

As a portfolio risk backed by amortizing cash flows - and unlike general corporate debt - the credit quality of securitized debt is non-stationary due to changes in volatility that are time- and structure-dependent.

a. Market value
c. Cross-border leasing
b. Debtor
d. Securitization

49. A _____ means that a company sells a product and agrees to buy it back after some time. If buyback price covers all costs of the inventory plus related holding costs, the inventory remains on the seller's books. In plain: there was no sale.

a. 3M Company
c. Buyback agreement
b. Modified Accelerated Cost Recovery System
d. BMC Software, Inc.

50. _____ is the risk of loss due to a debtor's non-payment of a loan or other line of credit (either the principal or interest (coupon) or both)

Most lenders employ their own models (credit scorecards) to rank potential and existing customers according to risk, and then apply appropriate strategies. With products such as unsecured personal loans or mortgages, lenders charge a higher price for higher risk customers and vice versa. With revolving products such as credit cards and overdrafts, risk is controlled through the setting of credit limits.

a. 3M Company
c. Currency risk
b. Market risk
d. Credit risk

Chapter 7. Cash and Receivables, 63

51. _____ means the giving out of information, either voluntarily or to be in compliance with legal regulations or workplace rules.

- In Computer security, full _____ means disclosing full information about vulnerabilities.
- In computing, _____ widget
- Journalism, full _____ refers to disclosing the interests of the writer which may bear on the subject being written about, for example, if the writer has worked with an interview subject in the past.

- In law:
    - The law of England and Wales, _____ refers to a process that may form part of legal proceedings, whereby parties inform to other parties the existence of any relevant documents that are, or have been, in their control. This compares with the process known as discovery in the course of legal proceedings in the United States.
    - In U.S. civil procedure (litigation rules for civil cases), _____ is a stage prior to trial. In civil cases, each party must disclose to the opposing party the following: names of witnesses which it may use to support its side, copies of documents (or mere description of these documents) in its control which it may use to support its side, computation of damages claimed, and certain insurance information. _____ is related to, but technically prior to, the discovery stage.
    - In Company law (known as 'corporate law' in the United States), _____ refers to giving out information about public or limited companies or their officers, which might be kept secret if the company was a private company or a partnership.

- In real property transactions, _____ refers to providing to a buyer information known to the seller or broker/agent concerning the condition or other aspects of real property that would affect the property's value or desirability. These rules regarding what information must be disclosed, and whether the information must be disclosed even if a buyer does not ask, vary from one jurisdiction to the next.

a. Controlled Foreign Corporations
c. Disclosure
b. Tax harmonisation
d. Trailing

52. _____, also called fair price (in a commonplace conflation of the two distinct concepts), is a concept used in finance and economics, defined as a rational and unbiased estimate of the potential market price of a good, service, or asset, taking into account such objective factors as:

- acquisition/production/distribution costs, replacement costs, or costs of close substitutes
- actual utility at a given level of development of social productive capability
- supply vs. demand

and subjective factors such as

- risk characteristics
- cost of capital
- individually perceived utility

In accounting, _____ is used as an estimate of the market value of an asset (or liability) for which a market price cannot be determined (usually because there is no established market for the asset.) Under GAAP (FAS 157), _____ is the amount at which the asset could be bought or sold in a current transaction between willing parties, or transferred to an equivalent party, other than in a liquidation sale. This is used for assets whose carrying value is based on mark-to-market valuations; for assets carried at historical cost, the _____ of the asset is not used. One example of where _____ is an issue is a College kitchen with a cost of $2 million which was built 5 years ago.

a. Fair Value
b. BMC Software, Inc.
c. BNSF Railway
d. 3M Company

53. _____s are cash, evidence of an ownership interest in an entity or deliver, cash or another _____.

_____s can be categorized by form depending on whether they are cash instruments or derivative instruments:

- Cash instruments are _____s whose value is determined directly by markets. They can be divided into securities, which are readily transferable, and other cash instruments such as loans and deposits, where both borrower and lender have to agree on a transfer.
- Derivative instruments are _____s which derive their value from the value and characteristics of one or more underlying assets. They can be divided into exchange-traded derivatives and over-the-counter (OTC) derivatives.

Alternatively, _____s can be categorized by 'asset class' depending on whether they are equity based (reflecting ownership of the issuing entity) or debt based (reflecting a loan the investor has made to the issuing entity.) If it is debt, it can be further categorised into short term (less than one year) or long term.

Foreign Exchange instruments and transactions are neither debt nor equity based and belong in their own category.

a. Mark-to-market
b. Financial Instrument
c. Financial instruments
d. Market price

54. _____ are cash, evidence of an ownership interest in an entity, or a contractual right to receive, or deliver, cash or another financial instrument.

Chapter 7. Cash and Receivables, 65

_____ can be categorized by form depending on whether they are cash instruments or derivative instruments:

- Cash instruments are _____ whose value is determined directly by markets. They can be divided into securities, which are readily transferable, and other cash instruments such as loans and deposits, where both borrower and lender have to agree on a transfer.
- Derivative instruments are _____ which derive their value from the value and characteristics of one or more underlying assets. They can be divided into exchange-traded derivatives and over-the-counter (OTC) derivatives.

Alternatively, _____ can be categorized by 'asset class' depending on whether they are equity based (reflecting ownership of the issuing entity) or debt based (reflecting a loan the investor has made to the issuing entity.) If it is debt, it can be further categorised into short term (less than one year) or long term.

Foreign Exchange instruments and transactions are neither debt nor equity based and belong in their own category.

   a. Financial Instruments   b. Spot rate
   c. Market liquidity   d. Transfer agent

55. _____ is a concept that denotes the precise probability of specific eventualities. Technically, the notion of _____ is independent from the notion of value and, as such, eventualities may have both beneficial and adverse consequences. However, in general usage the convention is to focus only on potential negative impact to some characteristic of value that may arise from a future event.
   a. Discount factor   b. Discounting
   c. Risk adjusted return on capital   d. Risk

56. _____ is one of the accounting liquidity ratios, a financial ratio. This ratio measures the number of times, on average, receivables (e.g. Accounts Receivable) are collected during the period. A popular variant of the _____ is to convert it into an Average Collection Period in terms of days.
   a. Price-to-sales ratio   b. Capital
   c. Shrinkage   d. Receivable turnover ratio

57. A _____ is a deposit account held at a bank or other financial institution, for the purpose of securely and quickly providing frequent access to funds on demand, through a variety of different channels. Because money is available on demand these accounts are also referred to as demand accounts or demand deposit accounts.

They are meant neither for the purpose of earning interest nor for the purpose of savings, but for convenience of the business or personal client; hence they tend not to bear interest.

   a. Transactional account   b. Reserve requirement
   c. Variable rate mortgage   d. Prime rate

58. The _____ is a form of financial accounting system. The most common _____ is the petty cash system.

The _____ ensures that you must document how the petty cash is spent. In a petty cash system, petty cash dockets are written for each amount issued. So when all of these dockets are totalled at the end of the month and deducted from the opening petty cash float, the calculated value must agree with what is left in the petty cash float. Under the _____, only that which is recorded as spent is replenished.

    a. AIG
    b. AMEX
    c. Imprest system
    d. ABC Television Network

59. _____ is the process of matching and comparing figures from accounting records against those presented on a bank statement. Less any items which have no relation to the bank statement, the balance of the accounting ledger should reconcile (match) to the balance of the bank statement.

_____ allows companies or individuals to compare their account records to the bank's records of their account balance in order to uncover any possible discrepancies.

    a. Lower of Cost or Market
    b. Credit memo
    c. Bank reconciliation
    d. Bankruptcy prediction

60. An account statement or a _____ is a summary of all financial transactions occurring over a given period of time on a deposit account, a credit card, or any other type of account offered by a financial institution.

_____s are typically printed on one or several pieces of paper and either mailed directly to the account holder's address, or kept at the financial institution's local branch for pick-up. Certain ATMs offer the possibility to print, at any time, a condensed version of a _____.

    a. BMC Software, Inc.
    b. BNSF Railway
    c. Bank statement
    d. 3M Company

61. _____ refers to a category of criminal acts that involve making the unlawful use of checks in order to illegally acquire or borrow funds that do not exist within the account balance or account-holder's legal ownership. Most methods involve taking advantage of the float (the time between the negotiation of the cheque and its clearance at the cheque-writer's bank) to draw out these funds. Specific kinds of cheque fraud include cheque kiting, where funds are deposited before the end of the float period to cover the fraud, and paper hanging, where the float offers the opportunity to commit the crime but the account is never replenished.

    a. 3M Company
    b. BNSF Railway
    c. Check fraud
    d. BMC Software, Inc.

62. _____ is a method of evaluating an asset's worth when held in inventory, in the field of accounting. _____ is part of the Generally Accepted Accounting Principles that apply to valuing inventory, so as to not overstate or understate the value of inventory goods. Net realisable value is generally equal to the selling price of the inventory goods less the selling costs (completion and disposal).

    a. Revenue recognition
    b. BMC Software, Inc.
    c. Net realizable value
    d. 3M Company

63. eFunds' _____ is a check verification service and consumer credit reporting agency like Experian, Equifax and TransUnion. While most credit reporting agencies broker data about how a consumer handles credit relationships, _____ provides data related to how a consumer has handled deposit accounts at banking institutions.

Eighty percent of all commercial banks and credit unions in the United States use _____ as a step in the consumer checking or savings account application process.

a. BNSF Railway
c. 3M Company
b. BMC Software, Inc.
d. ChexSystems

64. Procter is a surname, and may also refer to:

- Bryan Waller Procter (pseud. Barry Cornwall), English poet
- Goodwin Procter, American law firm
- _____, consumer products multinational

a. Welfare
c. Screening
b. Markup
d. Procter ' Gamble

Chapter 8. Valuation of Inventories: A Cost-Basis Approach,

1. A _____ is the pinnacle activity involved in selling products or services in return for money or other compensation. It is an act of completion of a commercial activity.

A _____ is completed by the seller, the owner of the goods.

a. Maturity
b. Tertiary sector of economy
c. High yield stock
d. Sale

2. The Exxon Mobil Corporation is an American oil and gas corporation. It is a direct descendant of John D. Rockefeller's Standard Oil company, formed on November 30, 1999, by the merger of Exxon and Mobil.

_____ is the world's largest publicly traded company when measured by either revenue or market capitalization.

a. ExxonMobil
b. Arthur Betz Laffer
c. Alan Greenspan
d. Abby Joseph Cohen

3. The _____ founded on April 1, 2001 is the successor of the International Accounting Standards Committee (IASC) founded in June 1973 in London. It is responsible for developing the International Financial Reporting Standards (new name for the International Accounting Standards issued after 2001), and promoting the use and application of these standards.

The _____ is an independent, privately-funded accounting standard-setter based in London, UK.

a. Information Systems Audit and Control Association
b. Emerging technologies
c. Institute of Management Accountants
d. International Accounting Standards Board

4. _____ refers to the methods, practices and operations conducted to promote and sustain certain categories of commercial activity. The term is understood to have different specific meanings depending on the context. Merchandise is a sale goods at a store

In marketing, one of the definitions of _____ is the practice in which the brand or image from one product or service is used to sell another.

a. BMC Software, Inc.
b. 3M Company
c. Merchandising
d. Merchandise

5. Procter is a surname, and may also refer to:

- Bryan Waller Procter (pseud. Barry Cornwall), English poet
- Goodwin Procter, American law firm
- _____, consumer products multinational

a. Welfare
b. Screening
c. Procter ' Gamble
d. Markup

Chapter 8. Valuation of Inventories: A Cost-Basis Approach, 69

6. A _____ is something that is acted upon or used by or by human labour or industry, for use as a building material to create some product or structure. Often the term is used to denote material that came from nature and is in an unprocessed or minimally processed state. Iron ore, logs, and crude oil, would be examples.
  a. BNSF Railway
  b. 3M Company
  c. BMC Software, Inc.
  d. Raw material

7. _____ or in-process inventory includes the set at large of unfinished items for products in a production process. These items are not yet completed but either just being fabricated or waiting in a queue for further processing or in a buffer storage. The term is used in production and supply chain management.
  a. BMC Software, Inc.
  b. BNSF Railway
  c. 3M Company
  d. Work in process

8. In economics, business, retail, and accounting, a _____ is the value of money that has been used up to produce something, and hence is not available for use anymore. In economics, a _____ is an alternative that is given up as a result of a decision. In business, the _____ may be one of acquisition, in which case the amount of money expended to acquire it is counted as _____.
  a. Cost of quality
  b. Cost allocation
  c. Prime cost
  d. Cost

9. In financial accounting, _____ or cost of sales includes the direct costs attributable to the production of the goods sold by a company. This amount includes the materials cost used in creating the goods along with the direct labor costs used to produce the good. It excludes indirect expenses such as distribution costs and sales force costs.
  a. FIFO and LIFO accounting
  b. 3M Company
  c. Reorder point
  d. Cost of goods sold

10. _____ is a process where a business physically counts its entire inventory. A _____ may be mandated by financial accounting rules or the tax regulations to place an accurate value on the inventory, or the business may need to count inventory so component parts or raw materials can be restocked. Businesses may use several different tactics to minimize the disruption caused by _____.
  a. BNSF Railway
  b. BMC Software, Inc.
  c. 3M Company
  d. Physical inventory

11. _____ is that part of statistical practice concerned with the selection of individual observations intended to yield some knowledge about a population of concern, especially for the purposes of statistical inference. Each observation measures one or more properties (weight, location, etc.) of an observable entity enumerated to distinguish objects or individuals.
  a. Abby Joseph Cohen
  b. Arthur Betz Laffer
  c. Sampling
  d. Alan Greenspan

12. An _____ allows a company to provide a monetary value for items that make up their inventory. Inventories are usually the largest current asset of a business, and proper measurement of them is necessary to assure accurate financial statements. If inventory is not properly measured, expenses and revenues cannot be properly matched and a company could make poor business decisions.
  a. AMEX
  b. ABC Television Network
  c. AIG
  d. Inventory valuation

Chapter 8. Valuation of Inventories: A Cost-Basis Approach,

13. In finance, _____ is the process of estimating the potential market value of a financial asset or liability. They can be done on assets (for example, investments in marketable securities such as stocks, options, business enterprises, or intangible assets such as patents and trademarks) or on liabilities (e.g., Bonds issued by a company.) A _____ is required in many contexts including investment analysis, capital budgeting, merger and acquisition transactions, financial reporting, taxable events to determine the proper tax liability, and in litigation.
    - a. Disclosure
    - b. Vyborg Appeal
    - c. Daybook
    - d. Valuation

14. _____ is one of a series of accounting transactions dealing with the billing of customers who owe money to a person, company or organization for goods and services that have been provided to the customer. In most business entities this is typically done by generating an invoice and mailing or electronically delivering it to the customer, who in turn must pay it within an established timeframe called credit or payment terms.

    An example of a common payment term is Net 30, meaning payment is due in the amount of the invoice 30 days from the date of invoice.

    - a. Adjusting entries
    - b. Accrual
    - c. Accounts receivable
    - d. Accrued revenue

15. _____ or international commercial terms are a series of international sales terms widely used throughout the world. They are used to divide transaction costs and responsibilities between buyer and seller and reflect state-of-the-art transportation practices. They closely correspond to the U.N. Convention on Contracts for the International Sale of Goods.
    - a. Incoterms
    - b. AMEX
    - c. ABC Television Network
    - d. AIG

16. A _____ means that a company sells a product and agrees to buy it back after some time. If buyback price covers all costs of the inventory plus related holding costs, the inventory remains on the seller's books. In plain: there was no sale.
    - a. Modified Accelerated Cost Recovery System
    - b. Buyback agreement
    - c. BMC Software, Inc.
    - d. 3M Company

17. In finance, _____ also known as return on investment, rate of profit or sometimes just return, is the ratio of money gained or lost on an investment relative to the amount of money invested. The amount of money gained or lost may be referred to as interest, profit/loss, gain/loss, or net income/loss. The money invested may be referred to as the asset, capital, principal, or the cost basis of the investment.
    - a. Debt to capital ratio
    - b. Capital employed
    - c. Theoretical ex-rights price
    - d. Rate of return

18. _____ is the amount of inventory a company have in stock at the end of this fiscal year. It is closely related with _____ Cost, which is the amount of money spent to get these goods in stock. It should be calculated at the Lower of Cost or Market.
    - a. Inventory turnover ratio
    - b. ABC Television Network
    - c. AIG
    - d. Ending inventory

Chapter 8. Valuation of Inventories: A Cost-Basis Approach,

19. _____ principle is a cornerstone of accrual accounting together with matching principle. They both determine the accounting period, in which revenues and expenses are recognized. According to the principle, revenues are recognized when they are (1) realized or realizable, and are (2) earned (usually when goods are transferred or services rendered), no matter when cash is received.

   a. Net realizable value   b. 3M Company

   c. BMC Software, Inc.   d. Revenue Recognition

20. An _____ is generally a 'disposition of property where at least 1 payment is to be received after the close of the taxable year in which the disposition occurs.'

If a taxpayer realizes income (e.g., gain) from an _____, the income generally must be reported by the taxpayer under the 'installment method.' The 'installment method' is defined as 'a method under which the income recognized for any taxable year [.

   a. AMEX   b. ABC Television Network

   c. AIG   d. Installment Sale

21. _____ refers to a business or organization attempting to acquire goods or services to accomplish the goals of the enterprise. Though there are several organizations that attempt to set standards in the _____ process, processes can vary greatly between organizations. Typically the word e;_____e; is not used interchangeably with the word e;procuremente;, since procurement typically includes Expediting, Supplier Quality, and Traffic and Logistics (T'L) in addition to _____.

   a. Supply chain   b. Purchasing

   c. Consignor   d. Free port

22. _____ is the concept of adding accumulated interest back to the principal, so that interest is earned on interest from that moment on. The act of declaring interest to be principal is called compounding (i.e., interest is compounded.) A loan, for example, may have its interest compounded every month: in this case, a loan with $100 principal and 1% interest per month would have a balance of $101 at the end of the first month.

   a. Trademark   b. Compound interest

   c. Risk management   d. Kanban

23. _____ is a fee paid on borrowed assets. It is the price paid for the use of borrowed money , or, money earned by deposited funds .Assets that are sometimes lent with _____ include money, shares, consumer goods through hire purchase, major assets such as aircraft, and even entire factories in finance lease arrangements. The _____ is calculated upon the value of the assets in the same manner as upon money.

   a. AIG   b. Interest

   c. Insolvency   d. ABC Television Network

24. A _____ is the transfer of wealth from one party (such as a person or company) to another. A _____ is usually made in exchange for the provision of goods, services or both, or to fulfill a legal obligation.

The simplest and oldest form of _____ is barter, the exchange of one good or service for another.

Chapter 8. Valuation of Inventories: A Cost-Basis Approach,

a. BMC Software, Inc.
b. 3M Company
c. Payee
d. Payment

25. _____ are reductions to a basic price of goods or services. They can occur anywhere in the distribution channel, modifying either the manufacturer's list price (determined by the manufacturer and often printed on the package), the retail price (set by the retailer and often attached to the product with a sticker), or the list price (which is quoted to a potential buyer, usually in written form.) The market price (also called effective price) is the amount actually paid.
   a. Resale price maintenance
   b. Discounts and allowances
   c. Target costing
   d. Pricing

26. Discounting is a financial mechanism in which a debtor obtains the right to delay payments to a creditor, for a defined period of time, in exchange for a charge or fee. Essentially, the party that owes money in the present purchases the right to delay the payment until some future date. The _____, or charge, is simply the difference between the original amount owed in the present and the amount that has to be paid in the future to settle the debt.
   a. Risk aversion
   b. Discount factor
   c. Discounting
   d. Discount

27. The _____ is the former authoritative body of the American Institute of Certified Public Accountants (AICPA.) It was created by the American Institute of Certified Public Accountants in 1959 and issued pronouncements on accounting principles until 1973, when it was replaced by the Financial Accounting Standards Board (FASB.)

The _____ was disbanded in the hopes that the smaller, fully-independent FASB could more effectively create accounting standards.

   a. Accounting Principles Board
   b. American Payroll Association
   c. International Federation of Accountants
   d. Institute of Management Accountants

28. _____ were documents issued by the Committee on Accounting Procedure between 1938 and 1959 on various accounting problems. They were discontinued with the dissolution of the Committee in 1959 under a recommendation from the Special Committee on Research Program. In all, 51 bulletins were issued, however, the lack of binding authority over AICPA's membership reduced the influence of, and compliance with the content of the bulletins.
   a. AIG
   b. ABC Television Network
   c. Other postemployment benefits
   d. Accounting Research Bulletins

29. _____ is a process of attributing cost to particular cost centres. For example the wage of the driver of the purchasing department can be allocated to the purchasing department cost centre. It is not necessary to share the wage cost over several different cost centers.
   a. Variable cost
   b. Cost accounting
   c. Cost of quality
   d. Cost allocation

30. Under the average-cost method, it is assumed that the cost of inventory is based on the _____ of the goods available for sale during the period. _____ is computed by dividing the total cost of goods available for sale by the total units available for sale. This gives a weighted-average unit cost that is applied to the units in the ending inventory.
   a. AIG
   b. ABC Television Network
   c. Ending inventory
   d. Average cost

Chapter 8. Valuation of Inventories: A Cost-Basis Approach, 73

31. Under the _____, it is assumed that the cost of inventory is based on the average cost of the goods available for sale during the period. Average cost is computed by dividing the total cost of goods available for sale by the total units available for sale. This gives a weighted-average unit cost that is applied to the units in the ending inventory.

   a. AMEX
   b. AIG
   c. ABC Television Network
   d. Average-cost method

32. _____ methods are means of managing inventory and financial matters involving the money a company ties up within inventory of produced goods, raw materials, parts, components, or feed stocks. FIFO stands for first-in, first-out, meaning that the oldest inventory items are recorded as sold first. LIFO stands for last-in, first-out, meaning that the most recently purchased items are recorded as sold first.

   a. Reorder point
   b. FIFO and LIFO accounting
   c. Finished good
   d. 3M Company

33. The _____ is the national, professional association of CPAs in the United States, with more than 330,000 members, including CPAs in business and industry, public practice, government, and education; student affiliates; and international associates. It sets ethical standards for the profession and U.S. auditing standards for audits of private companies; federal, state and local governments; and non-profit organizations.

   Approximately 40% of its members are engaged in the practice of public accounting, in areas such as auditing, accounting, taxation, general business consulting, business valuation, personal financial planning and business technology.

   a. American Institute of Certified Public Accountants
   b. ABC Television Network
   c. AIG
   d. Other postemployment benefits

34. In law, _____ refers to the process by which a company (or part of a company) is brought to an end, and the assets and property of the company redistributed. _____ can also be referred to as winding-up or dissolution, although dissolution technically refers to the last stage of _____. The process of _____ also arises when customs, an authority or agency in a country responsible for collecting and safeguarding customs duties, determines the final computation or ascertainment of the duties or drawback accruing on an entry.

   a. Liquidation
   b. 3M Company
   c. Bankruptcy protection
   d. BMC Software, Inc.

35. The _____ is a financial ratio that measures whether or not a firm has enough resources to pay its debts over the next 12 months. It compares a firm's current assets to its current liabilities. It is expressed as follows:

$$\text{Current ratio} = \frac{\text{Current Assets}}{\text{Current Liabilities}}$$

For example, if WXY Company's current assets are $50,000,000 and its current liabilities are $40,000,000, then its _____ would be $50,000,000 divided by $40,000,000, which equals 1.25.

   a. Net Interest Income
   b. Times interest earned
   c. Return on capital
   d. Current ratio

Chapter 8. Valuation of Inventories: A Cost-Basis Approach,

36. _____ is an acronym for First In, First Out, an abstraction in ways of organizing and manipulation of data relative to time and prioritization. This expression describes the principle of a queue processing technique or servicing conflicting demands by ordering process by first-come, first-served (FCFS) behaviour: what comes in first is handled first, what comes in next waits until the first is finished, etc.

Thus it is analogous to the behaviour of persons queueing (or 'standing in line', in common American parlance), where the persons leave the queue in the order they arrive, or waiting one's turn at a traffic control signal.

   a. Risk management   b. Trademark
   c. Kanban   d. FIFO

37. _____ is a business, economics or investment term that refers to an asset's ability to be easily converted through an act of buying or selling without causing a significant movement in the price and with minimum loss of value. Money, or cash on hand, is the most liquid asset. An act of exchange of a less liquid asset with a more liquid asset is called liquidation.

   a. Spot rate   b. Transfer agent
   c. Financial instruments   d. Market liquidity

38. _____ is systematic determination of merit, worth, and significance of something or someone using criteria against a set of standards. _____ often is used to characterize and appraise subjects of interest in a wide range of human enterprises, including the arts, criminal justice, foundations and non-profit organizations, government, health care, and other human services.

Depending on the topic of interest, there are professional groups which look to the quality and rigor of the _____ process.

   a. AIG   b. ABC Television Network
   c. AMEX   d. Evaluation

39. _____ consists of the sale of goods or merchandise from a fixed location, such as a department store, boutique or kiosk in small or individual lots for direct consumption by the purchaser. _____ may include subordinated services, such as delivery. Purchasers may be individuals or businesses.

   a. BMC Software, Inc.   b. Retailing
   c. BNSF Railway   d. 3M Company

40. An _____ is a term used in behavioral economics to describe those types of behaviors that impose costs on a person in the long-run that are not taken into account when making decisions in the present. Classical Economics discourages government from creating legislation that targets internalities, because it is assumed that the consumer takes these personal costs into account when paying for the good that causes the _____. For example, cigarettes should be taxed because of the negative consumption externalities that they impose, such as second-hand smoke, not because the smoker harms him or herself by smoking.

   a. Authorised capital   b. Operating budget
   c. Internality   d. Inventory turnover ratio

41. _____ in economics and business is the result of an exchange and from that trade we assign a numerical monetary value to a good, service or asset. If Alice trades Bob 4 apples for an orange, the _____ of an orange is 4 apples. Inversely, the _____ of an apple is 1/4 oranges.

Chapter 8. Valuation of Inventories: A Cost-Basis Approach,

a. Price discrimination
c. Discounts and allowances
b. Transactional Net Margin Method
d. Price

42. The _____, a unit of the United States Department of Labor, is the principal fact-finding agency for the U.S. government in the broad field of labor economics and statistics. The _____ is an independent national statistical agency that collects, processes, analyzes, and disseminates essential statistical data to the American public, the U.S. Congress, other Federal agencies, State and local governments, business, and labor representatives.

a. 3M Company
c. BMC Software, Inc.
b. BNSF Railway
d. Bureau of Labor Statistics

43. The _____ is the United States federal government agency that collects taxes and enforces the internal revenue laws. It is an agency within the U.S. Dept of the treasury responsible for interpretation and application of Federal tax law. The official U.S. Treasury regulations provide (in part):

The _____ is a bureau of the Department of the Treasury under the immediate direction of the Commissioner of Internal Revenue.

a. Internal Revenue Service
c. Use tax
b. Indirect tax
d. Income tax

44. _____ is a mathematical science pertaining to the collection, analysis, interpretation or explanation, and presentation of data. It also provides tools for prediction and forecasting based on data. It is applicable to a wide variety of academic disciplines, from the natural and social sciences to the humanities, government and business.

a. Statistics
c. Variance
b. Time series
d. Probability distribution

45. _____ (NYSE: DE) is an American corporation based in Moline, Illinois, and the leading manufacturer of agricultural machinery in the world. In 2008, it was listed as 102nd in the Fortune 500 ranking. Deere and Company agricultural products, usually sold under the John Deere name, include tractors, combine harvesters, balers, planters/seeders, ATVs and forestry equipment.

a. Deere ' Company
c. Governmental Accounting Standards Board
b. Professional association
d. Freddie Mac

Chapter 9. Inventories: Additional Valuation Issues,

1. _____ was an American chain of discount department stores based in Rocky Hill, Connecticut, USA. The company was founded in 1958 with a store in Southbridge, Massachusetts and at its peak operated 700 stores in 20 states, including the Northeast, Upper South, Midwest and the District of Columbia, making it the fourth largest discount retailer in America.

Despite its successes in its later years _____ was plagued by debt and a slow decline in sales, which resulted in two bankruptcy filings and ultimately put an end to the chain as the company, despite expanding into other markets and taking over many stores that had been abandoned by competitors that had closed, went out of business in 2002.

a. Ames
b. AIG
c. ABC Television Network
d. AMEX

2. The _____ is the former authoritative body of the American Institute of Certified Public Accountants (AICPA.) It was created by the American Institute of Certified Public Accountants in 1959 and issued pronouncements on accounting principles until 1973, when it was replaced by the Financial Accounting Standards Board (FASB.)

The _____ was disbanded in the hopes that the smaller, fully-independent FASB could more effectively create accounting standards.

a. American Payroll Association
b. Accounting Principles Board
c. International Federation of Accountants
d. Institute of Management Accountants

3. _____ were documents issued by the Committee on Accounting Procedure between 1938 and 1959 on various accounting problems. They were discontinued with the dissolution of the Committee in 1959 under a recommendation from the Special Committee on Research Program. In all, 51 bulletins were issued, however, the lack of binding authority over AICPA's membership reduced the influence of, and compliance with the content of the bulletins.

a. Other postemployment benefits
b. ABC Television Network
c. AIG
d. Accounting Research Bulletins

4. In economics, business, retail, and accounting, a _____ is the value of money that has been used up to produce something, and hence is not available for use anymore. In economics, a _____ is an alternative that is given up as a result of a decision. In business, the _____ may be one of acquisition, in which case the amount of money expended to acquire it is counted as _____.

a. Prime cost
b. Cost allocation
c. Cost of quality
d. Cost

5. _____ is generally understood in financial circles as the point at which revenue is recognized, typically through a transaction which involves the exchange of an asset, product, or service for cash or its equivalents.

This approach gives the accounting division a strictly objective basis for changing the books. For example, a homeowner may believe that his house has grown in value during a strong market, or fallen in value during a weak market, but until the house is actually sold for a specific price to a specific buyer, the change in value can only be estimated and is considered unrealized.

a. Total-factor productivity
b. Merck ' Co., Inc.
c. Valuation
d. Realization

Chapter 9. Inventories: Additional Valuation Issues, 77

6. A _____ is any one of a variety of different systems, institutions, procedures, social relations and infrastructures whereby persons trade, and goods and services are exchanged, forming part of the economy. It is an arrangement that allows buyers and sellers to exchange things. _____s vary in size, range, geographic scale, location, types and variety of human communities, as well as the types of goods and services traded.

   a. Market Failure   b. Market

   c. Recession   d. Perfect competition

7. _____ is the price at which an asset would trade in a competitive Walrasian auction setting. _____ is often used interchangeably with open _____, fair value or fair _____, although these terms have distinct definitions in different standards, and may differ in some circumstances.

International Valuation Standards defines _____ as 'the estimated amount for which a property should exchange on the date of valuation between a willing buyer and a willing seller in an arme;s-length transaction after proper marketing wherein the parties had each acted knowledgeably, prudently, and without compulsion.'

_____ is a concept distinct from market price, which is e;the price at which one can transacte;, while _____ is e;the true underlying valuee; according to theoretical standards.

   a. Segregated portfolio company   b. Market value

   c. Sinking fund   d. Debtor

8. The _____ is the national, professional association of CPAs in the United States, with more than 330,000 members, including CPAs in business and industry, public practice, government, and education; student affiliates; and international associates. It sets ethical standards for the profession and U.S. auditing standards for audits of private companies; federal, state and local governments; and non-profit organizations.

Approximately 40% of its members are engaged in the practice of public accounting, in areas such as auditing, accounting, taxation, general business consulting, business valuation, personal financial planning and business technology.

   a. AIG   b. American Institute of Certified Public Accountants

   c. Other postemployment benefits   d. ABC Television Network

9. In financial accounting and finance, _____ is the portion of receivables that can no longer be collected, typically from accounts receivable or loans. _____ in accounting is considered an expense.

There are two methods to account for _____:

1. Direct write off method (Non - GAAP)

A receivable which is not considered collectible is charged directly to the income statement.

1. Allowance method (GAAP)

Chapter 9. Inventories: Additional Valuation Issues,

An estimate is made at the end of each fiscal year of the amount of _____. This is then accumulated in a provision which is then used to reduce specific receivable accounts as and when necessary.

- a. 3M Company
- b. Total Expense Ratio
- c. Bad debt
- d. Tax expense

10. _____ methods are means of managing inventory and financial matters involving the money a company ties up within inventory of produced goods, raw materials, parts, components, or feed stocks. FIFO stands for first-in, first-out, meaning that the oldest inventory items are recorded as sold first. LIFO stands for last-in, first-out, meaning that the most recently purchased items are recorded as sold first.

- a. 3M Company
- b. FIFO and LIFO accounting
- c. Finished good
- d. Reorder point

11. In law, _____ refers to the process by which a company (or part of a company) is brought to an end, and the assets and property of the company redistributed. _____ can also be referred to as winding-up or dissolution, although dissolution technically refers to the last stage of _____. The process of _____ also arises when customs, an authority or agency in a country responsible for collecting and safeguarding customs duties, determines the final computation or ascertainment of the duties or drawback accruing on an entry.

- a. BMC Software, Inc.
- b. Liquidation
- c. Bankruptcy protection
- d. 3M Company

12. An _____ allows a company to provide a monetary value for items that make up their inventory. Inventories are usually the largest current asset of a business, and proper measurement of them is necessary to assure accurate financial statements. If inventory is not properly measured, expenses and revenues cannot be properly matched and a company could make poor business decisions.

- a. AIG
- b. ABC Television Network
- c. Inventory valuation
- d. AMEX

13. _____ is a method of evaluating an asset's worth when held in inventory, in the field of accounting. _____ is part of the Generally Accepted Accounting Principles that apply to valuing inventory, so as to not overstate or understate the value of inventory goods. Net realisable value is generally equal to the selling price of the inventory goods less the selling costs (completion and disposal).

- a. Revenue recognition
- b. BMC Software, Inc.
- c. 3M Company
- d. Net realizable value

14. In finance, _____ is the process of estimating the potential market value of a financial asset or liability. They can be done on assets (for example, investments in marketable securities such as stocks, options, business enterprises, or intangible assets such as patents and trademarks) or on liabilities (e.g., Bonds issued by a company.) A _____ is required in many contexts including investment analysis, capital budgeting, merger and acquisition transactions, financial reporting, taxable events to determine the proper tax liability, and in litigation.

- a. Disclosure
- b. Vyborg Appeal
- c. Daybook
- d. Valuation

Chapter 9. Inventories: Additional Valuation Issues, 79

15. _____ is one of a series of accounting transactions dealing with the billing of customers who owe money to a person, company or organization for goods and services that have been provided to the customer. In most business entities this is typically done by generating an invoice and mailing or electronically delivering it to the customer, who in turn must pay it within an established timeframe called credit or payment terms.

An example of a common payment term is Net 30, meaning payment is due in the amount of the invoice 30 days from the date of invoice.

- a. Accounts receivable
- b. Adjusting entries
- c. Accrual
- d. Accrued revenue

16. A _____ is the pinnacle activity involved in selling products or services in return for money or other compensation. It is an act of completion of a commercial activity.

A _____ is completed by the seller, the owner of the goods.

- a. Tertiary sector of economy
- b. Sale
- c. High yield stock
- d. Maturity

17. _____ are formal records of a business' financial activities.

In British English, including United Kingdom company law, _____ are often referred to as accounts, although the term _____ is also used, particularly by accountants.

_____ provide an overview of a business' financial condition in both short and long term.

- a. Notes to the financial statements
- b. 3M Company
- c. Financial Statements
- d. Statement of retained earnings

18. In accounting, _____ or sales profit is the difference between revenue and the cost of making a product or providing a service, before deducting overhead, payroll, taxation, and interest payments. Note that this is different from operating profit (earnings before interest and taxes.)

Net sales are calculated:

Net sales = Sales - Sales returns and allowances.

- a. Gross profit
- b. Participating preferred stock
- c. Capital structure
- d. Commercial paper

19. _____ are standards and interpretations adopted by the International Accounting Standards Board (IASB.)

Many of the standards forming part of _____ are known by the older name of International Accounting Standards (IAS.) IAS were issued between 1973 and 2001 by the board of the International Accounting Standards Committee (IASC.)

Chapter 9. Inventories: Additional Valuation Issues,

a. International Financial Reporting Standards
b. Out-of-pocket
c. AIG
d. ABC Television Network

20. _____ is systematic determination of merit, worth, and significance of something or someone using criteria against a set of standards. _____ often is used to characterize and appraise subjects of interest in a wide range of human enterprises, including the arts, criminal justice, foundations and non-profit organizations, government, health care, and other human services.

Depending on the topic of interest, there are professional groups which look to the quality and rigor of the _____ process.

a. AIG
b. AMEX
c. ABC Television Network
d. Evaluation

21. _____, Gross profit margin or Gross Profit Rate can be defined as the amount of contribution to the business enterprise, after paying for direct-fixed and direct-variable unit costs, required to cover overheads (fixed commitments) and provide a buffer for unknown items. It expresses the relationship between gross profit and sales revenue.

It can be expressed in absolute terms:

Gross Profit = Revenue − Cost of Goods Sold

or as the ratio of gross profit to sales revenue, usually in the form of a percentage:

_____ Percentage = (Revenue-Cost of Goods Sold)/Revenue

Cost of goods sold includes variable costs and fixed costs directly linked to the product, such as material and labor.

a. 3M Company
b. BNSF Railway
c. BMC Software, Inc.
d. Gross margin

22. _____ is the calculated approximation of a result which is usable even if input data may be incomplete or uncertain.

In statistics, see _____ theory, estimator.

In mathematics, approximation or _____ typically means finding upper or lower bounds of a quantity that cannot readily be computed precisely and is also an educated guess .

a. Estimation
b. ABC Television Network
c. AIG
d. AMEX

Chapter 9. Inventories: Additional Valuation Issues,

23. _____ is the difference between the cost of a good or service and its selling price. A _____ is added on to the total cost incurred by the producer of a good or service in order to create a profit. The total cost reflects the total amount of both fixed and variable expenses to produce and distribute a product.
    a. Merck ' Co., Inc.
    b. Corporate Bond
    c. Statements of Financial Accounting Standards No. 133, Accounting for Derivative Instruments and Hedging Activities
    d. Markup

24. _____ in economics and business is the result of an exchange and from that trade we assign a numerical monetary value to a good, service or asset. If Alice trades Bob 4 apples for an orange, the _____ of an orange is 4 apples. Inversely, the _____ of an apple is 1/4 oranges.
    a. Price
    b. Price discrimination
    c. Transactional Net Margin Method
    d. Discounts and allowances

25. _____ is a lightweight markup language, originally created by John Gruber and Aaron Swartz to help maximum readability and 'publishability' of both its input and output forms. The language takes many cues from existing conventions for marking up plain text in email. _____ converts its marked-up text input to valid, well-formed XHTML and replaces left-pointing angle brackets ('<') and ampersands with their corresponding character entity references.
    a. BMC Software, Inc.
    b. BNSF Railway
    c. Markdown
    d. 3M Company

26. _____ consists of the sale of goods or merchandise from a fixed location, such as a department store, boutique or kiosk in small or individual lots for direct consumption by the purchaser. _____ may include subordinated services, such as delivery. Purchasers may be individuals or businesses.
    a. BMC Software, Inc.
    b. 3M Company
    c. BNSF Railway
    d. Retailing

27. Discounting is a financial mechanism in which a debtor obtains the right to delay payments to a creditor, for a defined period of time, in exchange for a charge or fee. Essentially, the party that owes money in the present purchases the right to delay the payment until some future date. The _____, or charge, is simply the difference between the original amount owed in the present and the amount that has to be paid in the future to settle the debt.
    a. Discounting
    b. Discount factor
    c. Risk aversion
    d. Discount

28. Employment is a contract between two parties, one being the employer and the other being the _____. An _____ may be defined as: 'A person in the service of another under any contract of hire, express or implied, oral or written, where the employer has the power or right to control and direct the _____ in the material details of how the work is to be performed.' Black's Law Dictionary page 471 (5th ed. 1979.)
    a. AIG
    b. AMEX
    c. ABC Television Network
    d. Employee

29. _____ is the process of understanding the stock/product mix combined with the knowledge of the demand for stock/product.
    a. AIG
    b. AMEX
    c. ABC Television Network
    d. Inventory analysis

30. The _____ is an equation that equals the cost of goods sold divided by the average inventory. Average inventory equals beginning inventory plus ending inventory divided by 2.

The formula for _____:

$$\text{Inventory Turnover} = \frac{\text{Cost of Goods Sold}}{\text{Average Inventory}}$$

The formula for average inventory:

$$\text{Average Inventory} = \frac{\text{Beginning inventory} + \text{Ending inventory}}{2}$$

A low turnover rate may point to overstocking, obsolescence, or deficiencies in the product line or marketing effort.

a. Enterprise Value/Sales
b. Upside potential ratio
c. Inventory turnover
d. Earnings per share

31. _____ is one of the Accounting Liquidity ratios, a financial ratio. This ratio measures the number of times, on average, the inventory is sold during the period. Its purpose is to measure the liquidity of the inventory.
a. ABC Television Network
b. Ending inventory
c. AIG
d. Inventory turnover ratio

32. An _____ is a term used in behavioral economics to describe those types of behaviors that impose costs on a person in the long-run that are not taken into account when making decisions in the present. Classical Economics discourages government from creating legislation that targets internalities, because it is assumed that the consumer takes these personal costs into account when paying for the good that causes the _____. For example, cigarettes should be taxed because of the negative consumption externalities that they impose, such as second-hand smoke, not because the smoker harms him or herself by smoking.
a. Inventory turnover ratio
b. Operating budget
c. Authorised capital
d. Internality

33. The _____ is the United States federal government agency that collects taxes and enforces the internal revenue laws. It is an agency within the U.S. Dept of the treasury responsible for interpretation and application of Federal tax law. The official U.S. Treasury regulations provide (in part):

The _____ is a bureau of the Department of the Treasury under the immediate direction of the Commissioner of Internal Revenue.

a. Income tax
c. Indirect tax

b. Use tax
d. Internal Revenue Service

34. Procter is a surname, and may also refer to:

- Bryan Waller Procter (pseud. Barry Cornwall), English poet
- Goodwin Procter, American law firm
- _____, consumer products multinational

a. Procter ' Gamble
c. Markup

b. Welfare
d. Screening

Chapter 10. Acquisition and Disposition of Property, Plant, and Equipment,

1. In probability theory and statistics, the _____ (or expectation value or mean and for continuous random variables with a density function it is the probability density -weighted integral of the possible values.

The term '_____' can be misleading.

   a. Expected value
   b. ABC Television Network
   c. AMEX
   d. AIG

2. _____, also known as property, plant, and equipment (PP&E), is a term used in accountancy for assets and property which cannot easily be converted into cash. This can be compared with current assets such as cash or bank accounts, which are described as liquid assets. In most cases, only tangible assets are referred to as fixed.
   a. Subledger
   b. Minority interest
   c. Bankruptcy prediction
   d. Fixed asset

3. _____ is any physical or virtual entity that is owned by an individual or jointly by a group of individuals. An owner of _____ has the right to consume, sell, rent, mortgage, transfer and exchange his or her _____. Important widely-recognized types of _____ include real _____, personal _____ (other physical possessions), and intellectual _____ (rights over artistic creations, inventions, etc.), although the latter is not always as widely recognized or enforced.
   a. Disclosure requirement
   b. Primary authority
   c. Fiduciary
   d. Property

4. In business and accounting, _____ are everything of value that is owned by a person or company. It is a claim on the property your income of a borrower. The balance sheet of a firm records the monetary value of the _____ owned by the firm.
   a. Earnings before interest, taxes, depreciation and amortization
   b. Accounts receivable
   c. Accrual basis accounting
   d. Assets

5. _____ were published by Accounting Principles Board (APB.) The board was created by American Institute of Certified Public Accountants (AICPA) in 1959 and was replaced by Financial Accounting Standards Board (FASB) in 1973. Its mission was to develop an overall conceptual framework of US generally accepted accounting principles (US GAAP.)
   a. ABC Television Network
   b. AIG
   c. Accounting Principles Board Opinions
   d. AMEX

6. An _____ is the buying of one company by another. An _____ may be friendly or hostile. In the former case, the companies cooperate in negotiations; in the latter case, the takeover target is unwilling to be bought or the target's board has no prior knowledge of the offer. _____ usually refers to a purchase of a smaller firm by a larger one. Sometimes, however, a smaller firm will acquire management control of a larger or longer established company and keep its name for the combined entity. This is known as a reverse takeover.
   a. ABC Television Network
   b. AMEX
   c. Acquisition
   d. AIG

7. In economics, business, retail, and accounting, a _____ is the value of money that has been used up to produce something, and hence is not available for use anymore. In economics, a _____ is an alternative that is given up as a result of a decision. In business, the _____ may be one of acquisition, in which case the amount of money expended to acquire it is counted as _____.

Chapter 10. Acquisition and Disposition of Property, Plant, and Equipment, 85

a. Prime cost
b. Cost of quality
c. Cost allocation
d. Cost

8. In finance, _____ is the process of estimating the potential market value of a financial asset or liability. They can be done on assets (for example, investments in marketable securities such as stocks, options, business enterprises, or intangible assets such as patents and trademarks) or on liabilities (e.g., Bonds issued by a company.) A _____ is required in many contexts including investment analysis, capital budgeting, merger and acquisition transactions, financial reporting, taxable events to determine the proper tax liability, and in litigation.

a. Vyborg Appeal
b. Disclosure
c. Daybook
d. Valuation

9. In business, _____, Overhead cost or _____ expense refers to an ongoing expense of operating a business. The term _____ is usually used to group expenses that are necessary to the continued functioning of the business, but do not directly generate profits.

_____ expenses are all costs on the income statement except for direct labor and direct materials.

a. Intangible assets
b. ABC Television Network
c. AIG
d. Overhead

10. _____ is an adverb or adjective, meaning in proportion. The term is used in many legal and economic contexts, and sometimes spelled pro-rata.

More specifically, _____ means:

1. In proportion to some factor that can be exactly calculated.
2. To count based on amount of time that has passed out of the total time.
3. Proportional Ratio

Pro-rata has a Latin etymology, from pro, according to, for, or by, and rata, feminine ablative of calculated .

Examples in law and economics include the following noted below.

a. Pro rata
b. BNSF Railway
c. 3M Company
d. BMC Software, Inc.

11. _____ is a fee paid on borrowed assets. It is the price paid for the use of borrowed money , or, money earned by deposited funds .Assets that are sometimes lent with _____ include money, shares, consumer goods through hire purchase, major assets such as aircraft, and even entire factories in finance lease arrangements. The _____ is calculated upon the value of the assets in the same manner as upon money.

a. AIG
b. ABC Television Network
c. Insolvency
d. Interest

Chapter 10. Acquisition and Disposition of Property, Plant, and Equipment,

12. _____ is the concept of adding accumulated interest back to the principal, so that interest is earned on interest from that moment on. The act of declaring interest to be principal is called compounding (i.e., interest is compounded.) A loan, for example, may have its interest compounded every month: in this case, a loan with $100 principal and 1% interest per month would have a balance of $101 at the end of the first month.

a. Risk management
b. Trademark
c. Kanban
d. Compound interest

13. _____ is the term used to refer to the standard framework of guidelines for financial accounting used in any given jurisdiction. _____ includes the standards, conventions, and rules accountants follow in recording and summarizing transactions, and in the preparation of financial statements.

Financial accounting information must be assembled and reported objectively.

a. Current asset
b. General ledger
c. Generally accepted accounting principles
d. Long-term liabilities

14. An _____ is the price a borrower pays for the use of money they do not own, for instance a small company might borrow from a bank to kick start their business, and the return a lender receives for deferring the use of funds, by lending it to the borrower. _____s are normally expressed as a percentage rate over the period of one year.

_____s targets are also a vital tool of monetary policy and are used to control variables like investment, inflation, and unemployment.

a. AIG
b. AMEX
c. ABC Television Network
d. Interest rate

15. _____ are reductions to a basic price of goods or services. They can occur anywhere in the distribution channel, modifying either the manufacturer's list price (determined by the manufacturer and often printed on the package), the retail price (set by the retailer and often attached to the product with a sticker), or the list price (which is quoted to a potential buyer, usually in written form.) The market price (also called effective price) is the amount actually paid.

a. Resale price maintenance
b. Target costing
c. Pricing
d. Discounts and allowances

16. Discounting is a financial mechanism in which a debtor obtains the right to delay payments to a creditor, for a defined period of time, in exchange for a charge or fee. Essentially, the party that owes money in the present purchases the right to delay the payment until some future date. The _____, or charge, is simply the difference between the original amount owed in the present and the amount that has to be paid in the future to settle the debt.

a. Discount factor
b. Discounting
c. Risk aversion
d. Discount

17. A _____ is a one-time payment of money, as opposed to a series of payments made over time.

a. Manufacturing operations
b. Lump sum
c. Redemption value
d. Trade name

Chapter 10. Acquisition and Disposition of Property, Plant, and Equipment,

18. _____ in economics and business is the result of an exchange and from that trade we assign a numerical monetary value to a good, service or asset. If Alice trades Bob 4 apples for an orange, the _____ of an orange is 4 apples. Inversely, the _____ of an apple is 1/4 oranges.

   a. Price discrimination
   b. Transactional Net Margin Method
   c. Discounts and allowances
   d. Price

19. _____ refers to a business or organization attempting to acquire goods or services to accomplish the goals of the enterprise. Though there are several organizations that attempt to set standards in the _____ process, processes can vary greatly between organizations. Typically the word e;_____e; is not used interchangeably with the word e;procuremente;, since procurement typically includes Expediting, Supplier Quality, and Traffic and Logistics (T'L) in addition to _____.

   a. Free port
   b. Consignor
   c. Supply chain
   d. Purchasing

20. _____ is a term used in accounting, economics and finance to spread the cost of an asset over the span of several years.

In simple words we can say that _____ is the reduction in the value of an asset due to usage, passage of time, wear and tear, technological outdating or obsolescence, depletion, inadequacy, rot, rust, decay or other such factors.

In accounting, _____ is a term used to describe any method of attributing the historical or purchase cost of an asset across its useful life, roughly corresponding to normal wear and tear.

   a. Current asset
   b. Net profit
   c. General ledger
   d. Depreciation

21. The _____ is one of three major groups of methodologies, called valuation approaches, used by appraisers. It is particularly common in commercial real estate appraisal and in business appraisal. The fundamental math is similar to the methods used for financial valuation, securities analysis, or bond pricing.

While there are quite a few acceptable methods under the rubric of the _____, most of these methods fall into three categories: direct capitalization, discounted cash flow, and gross income multiplier.

   a. Income approach
   b. AIG
   c. AMEX
   d. ABC Television Network

22. A _____ is any one of a variety of different systems, institutions, procedures, social relations and infrastructures whereby persons trade, and goods and services are exchanged, forming part of the economy. It is an arrangement that allows buyers and sellers to exchange things. _____s vary in size, range, geographic scale, location, types and variety of human communities, as well as the types of goods and services traded.

   a. Market Failure
   b. Perfect competition
   c. Recession
   d. Market

Chapter 10. Acquisition and Disposition of Property, Plant, and Equipment,

23. _____, also called fair price (in a commonplace conflation of the two distinct concepts), is a concept used in finance and economics, defined as a rational and unbiased estimate of the potential market price of a good, service, or asset, taking into account such objective factors as:

- acquisition/production/distribution costs, replacement costs, or costs of close substitutes
- actual utility at a given level of development of social productive capability
- supply vs. demand

and subjective factors such as

- risk characteristics
- cost of capital
- individually perceived utility

In accounting, _____ is used as an estimate of the market value of an asset (or liability) for which a market price cannot be determined (usually because there is no established market for the asset.) Under GAAP (FAS 157), _____ is the amount at which the asset could be bought or sold in a current transaction between willing parties, or transferred to an equivalent party, other than in a liquidation sale. This is used for assets whose carrying value is based on mark-to-market valuations; for assets carried at historical cost, the _____ of the asset is not used. One example of where _____ is an issue is a College kitchen with a cost of $2 million which was built 5 years ago.

a. BMC Software, Inc.
b. 3M Company
c. BNSF Railway
d. Fair Value

24. In economics, _____ or _____ goods or real _____ refers to factors of production used to create goods or services that are not themselves significantly consumed (though they may depreciate) in the production process. _____ goods may be acquired with money or financial _____. In finance and accounting, _____ generally refers to financial wealth, especially that used to start or maintain a business.

a. Disclosure
b. Vyborg Appeal
c. Screening
d. Capital

25. A _____ is an expenditure creating future benefits. A _____ is incurred when a business spends money either to buy fixed assets or to add to the value of an existing fixed asset with a useful life that extends beyond the taxable year. Capex are used by a company to acquire or upgrade physical assets such as equipment, property, or industrial buildings.

a. Cost of capital
b. Capital expenditure
c. BMC Software, Inc.
d. 3M Company

26. In accounting, _____ has a very specific meaning. It is an outflow of cash or other valuable assets from a person or company to another person or company. This outflow of cash is generally one side of a trade for products or services that have equal or better current or future value to the buyer than to the seller.

a. AMEX
b. AIG
c. ABC Television Network
d. Expense

Chapter 10. Acquisition and Disposition of Property, Plant, and Equipment, 89

27. An _____, operating expenditure, operational expense, operational expenditure or OPEX is an on-going cost for running a product, business, or system. Its counterpart, a capital expenditure (CAPEX), is the cost of developing or providing non-consumable parts for the product or system. For example, the purchase of a photocopier is the CAPEX, and the annual paper and toner cost is the OPEX.

    a. AIG   b. AMEX
    c. ABC Television Network   d. Operating expense

28. _____ refers to services paid for in advance. Examples include tolls, pay as you go cell phones, and stored-value cards such as gift cards and preloaded credit cards. _____ accounts are assets, and they are increased by debiting the account(s.)

    a. Prepaid   b. 3M Company
    c. BNSF Railway   d. BMC Software, Inc.

29. _____ is fixing any sort of mechanical or electrical device should it become out of order or broken (known as repair or unscheduled maintenance) as well as performing the routine actions which keep the device in working order (known as scheduled maintenance) or prevent trouble from arising (preventive maintenance.) The MRO business is seeing a major boom with the emergence of international carriers and private aviation in Asia. The MRO business in India alone is expected to grow to $45Bn from the current $0.5Bn in the next decade.

    a. 3M Company   b. BNSF Railway
    c. Maintenance, repair and operations   d. BMC Software, Inc.

30. A _____ is a habit, a preparation, a state of readiness, or a tendency to act in a specified way.

The terms dispositional belief and occurrent belief refer, in the former case, to a belief that is held in the mind but not currently being considered, and in the latter case, to a belief that is currently being considered by the mind.

In Bourdieu's theory of fields _____s are the natural tendencies of each individual to take on a certain position in any field.

    a. BNSF Railway   b. 3M Company
    c. Disposition   d. BMC Software, Inc.

31. A _____ is the pinnacle activity involved in selling products or services in return for money or other compensation. It is an act of completion of a commercial activity.

A _____ is completed by the seller, the owner of the goods.

    a. Tertiary sector of economy   b. Maturity
    c. High yield stock   d. Sale

Chapter 11. Depreciation, Impairments, and Depletion,

1. _____ is the collection, transport, processing, recycling or disposal, and monitoring of waste materials. The term usually relates to materials produced by human activity, and is generally undertaken to reduce their effect on health, the environment or aesthetics. _____ is also carried out to recover resources from it.

   a. BNSF Railway
   b. Waste Management
   c. 3M Company
   d. BMC Software, Inc.

2. The term _____ describes a reduction in recognized value. In accounting terminology, it refers to recognition of the reduced or zero value of an asset. In income tax statements, it refers to a reduction of taxable income as recognition of certain expenses required to produce the income.

   a. Write-off
   b. Payroll
   c. Salvage value
   d. Current asset

3. Book Value = Original Cost - _____

Book value at the end of year becomes book value at the beginning of next year. The asset is depreciated until the book value equals scrap value.

If the vehicle were to be sold and the sales price exceeded the depreciated value (net book value) then the excess would be considered a gain and subject to depreciation recapture.

   a. Accumulated Depreciation
   b. ABC Television Network
   c. AIG
   d. AMEX

4. _____ is the process of increasing, or accounting for, an amount over a period of time. Particular instances of the term include:

   - _____, the allocation of a lump sum amount to different time periods, particularly for loans and other forms of finance, including related interest or other finance charges.
     - _____ schedule, a table detailing each periodic payment on a loan (typically a mortgage), as generated by an _____ calculator.
     - Negative _____, an _____ schedule where the loan amount actually increases through not paying the full interest
   - Amortized analysis, analyzing the execution cost of algorithms over a sequence of operations.
   - _____ of capital expenditures of certain assets under accounting rules, particularly intangible assets, in a manner analogous to depreciation.
   - _____

   a. EBIT
   b. Annuity
   c. Intangible
   d. Amortization

5. In economics, business, retail, and accounting, a _____ is the value of money that has been used up to produce something, and hence is not available for use anymore. In economics, a _____ is an alternative that is given up as a result of a decision. In business, the _____ may be one of acquisition, in which case the amount of money expended to acquire it is counted as _____.

   a. Cost
   b. Cost allocation
   c. Prime cost
   d. Cost of quality

Chapter 11. Depreciation, Impairments, and Depletion,

6. _____ is a process of attributing cost to particular cost centres. For example the wage of the driver of the purchasing department can be allocated to the purchasing department cost centre. It is not necessary to share the wage cost over several different cost centers.

   a. Variable cost
   b. Cost accounting
   c. Cost allocation
   d. Cost of quality

7. _____ is a term used in accounting, economics and finance to spread the cost of an asset over the span of several years.

In simple words we can say that _____ is the reduction in the value of an asset due to usage, passage of time, wear and tear, technological outdating or obsolescence, depletion, inadequacy, rot, rust, decay or other such factors.

In accounting, _____ is a term used to describe any method of attributing the historical or purchase cost of an asset across its useful life, roughly corresponding to normal wear and tear.

   a. General ledger
   b. Net profit
   c. Current asset
   d. Depreciation

8. _____ was founded in 1898 by Frank Seiberling. Today it is the third largest tire company in the world after Bridgestone and Michelin. Goodyear manufactures tires for automobiles, commercial trucks, light trucks, SUVs, race cars, airplanes, and heavy earth-mover machinery.

   a. Factor
   b. Fiscal
   c. Trailing
   d. The Goodyear Tire ' Rubber Company

9. In finance, a _____ is a debt security, in which the authorized issuer owes the holders a debt and, depending on the terms of the _____, is obliged to pay interest (the coupon) and/or to repay the principal at a later date, termed maturity. It is a formal contract to repay borrowed money with interest at fixed intervals.

Thus a _____ is like a loan: the issuer is the borrower, the _____ holder is the lender, and the coupon is the interest.

   a. Revenue bonds
   b. Zero-coupon bond
   c. Bond
   d. Coupon rate

10. In business and accounting, _____ are everything of value that is owned by a person or company. It is a claim on the property your income of a borrower. The balance sheet of a firm records the monetary value of the _____ owned by the firm.

   a. Accounts receivable
   b. Assets
   c. Accrual basis accounting
   d. Earnings before interest, taxes, depreciation and amortization

11. Straight-line depreciation is the simplest and most often used technique, in which the company estimates the _____ of the asset at the end of the period during which it will be used to generate revenues (useful life), and will expense a portion of original cost in equal increments over that period. The _____ is an estimate of the value of the asset at the time it will be sold or disposed of; it may be zero. _____ is scrap value, by another name.

Chapter 11. Depreciation, Impairments, and Depletion,

a. Net profit
b. Generally accepted accounting principles
c. Closing entries
d. Salvage value

12. In financial accounting, a _____ or statement of financial position is a summary of a person's or organization's balances. Assets, liabilities and ownership equity are listed as of a specific date, such as the end of its financial year. A _____ is often described as a snapshot of a company's financial condition.

a. Statement of retained earnings
b. Balance sheet
c. 3M Company
d. Financial statements

13. In mathematics _____s are numbers or other things that get multiplied. In particular, see:

- Factorization, the decomposition of an object into a product of other objects
- Integer factorization, the process of breaking down a composite number into smaller non-trivial divisors
- A coefficient
- A divisor of a particular number, or of an element of a monoid
- A von Neumann algebra with a trivial center

In statistics

- _____ analysis is the study of how _____s or certain variables affect variables.

In technology:

- Human _____s, a profession that focuses on how people interact with products, tools, or procedures
- 'Functionality, Application domain, Conditions, Technology, Objects and Responsibility;', In object-oriented programming

In computer science and information technology:

- Authentication _____, a piece of information used to verify a person's identity for security purposes
- _____, a Unix command for numbers factorization
- _____ (programming language), an experimental Forth-like programming language

In television:

- The O'Reilly _____, an American talk show hosted by Bill O'Reilly on Fox News.
- The Krypton _____, a British game show hosted by Gordon Burns, formally on ITV. Also had an American version.

a. The Goodyear Tire ' Rubber Company
b. Valuation
c. Merck ' Co., Inc.
d. Factor

14. _____ is a non-GAAP metric that can be used to evaluate a company's profitability.

Chapter 11. Depreciation, Impairments, and Depletion,

EBITDA = Operating Revenue - Operating Expenses + Other Revenue

Its name comes from the fact that Operating Expenses do not include interest, taxes, or amortization. _____ is not a defined measure according to Generally Accepted Accounting Principles (GAAP) and thus can be calculated however a company wishes.

a. Earnings before interest, taxes, depreciation and amortization
b. Accrued expense
c. Accrual
d. Accounts receivable

15. _____ is a specific term used in companies' financial reporting from the company-whole point of view. Because that use excludes the effects of changing ownership interest, an economic measure of _____ is necessary for financial analysis from the shareholders' point of view

_____ is defined by the Financial Accounting Standards Board, or FASB, as 'the change in equity [net assets] of a business enterprise during a period from transactions and other events and circumstances from nonowner sources. It includes all changes in equity during a period except those resulting from investments by owners and distributions to owners.'

_____ is the sum of net income and other items that must bypass the income statement because they have not been realized, including items like an unrealized holding gain or loss from available for sale securities and foreign currency translation gains or losses.

a. BMC Software, Inc.
b. BNSF Railway
c. 3M Company
d. Comprehensive income

16. _____ is a fee paid on borrowed assets. It is the price paid for the use of borrowed money , or, money earned by deposited funds .Assets that are sometimes lent with _____ include money, shares, consumer goods through hire purchase, major assets such as aircraft, and even entire factories in finance lease arrangements. The _____ is calculated upon the value of the assets in the same manner as upon money.

a. Insolvency
b. AIG
c. ABC Television Network
d. Interest

17. There are several methods for calculating depreciation, generally based on either the passage of time or the level of activity (or use) of the asset.

_____ is the simplest and most often used technique, in which the company estimates the salvage value of the asset at the end of the period during which it will be used to generate revenues (useful life), and will expense a portion of original cost in equal increments over that period.

a. Straight-line depreciation
b. Pro forma
c. Current asset
d. Closing entries

Chapter 11. Depreciation, Impairments, and Depletion,

18. A _____ or _____ is a tax designation for a corporation investing in real estate that reduces or eliminates corporate income taxes. In return, _____s are required to distribute 90% of their income, which may be taxable in the hands of the investors. The _____ structure was designed to provide a similar structure for investment in real estate as mutual funds provide for investment in stocks.
   a. Real Estate Investment Trust
   b. Liquidation value
   c. 3M Company
   d. REIT

19. A _____ is a tax designation for a corporation investing in real estate that reduces or eliminates corporate income taxes. In return, _____s are required to distribute 90% of their income, which may be taxable in the hands of the investors. The _____ structure was designed to provide a similar structure for investment in real estate as mutual funds provide for investment in stocks.
   a. 3M Company
   b. Real Estate Investment Trust
   c. REIT
   d. Liquidation value

20. In tax accounting the _____ is the default applicable convention used for federal income tax purposes. Like other conventions, the _____ affects the depreciation deduction computation in the year in which the property is placed into service. Using the _____, a taxpayer claims a half of a year's depreciation for the first taxable year, regardless of when the property was actually put into service.
   a. Reverse Morris trust
   b. Taxable income
   c. Revenue Procedures
   d. Half-year convention

21. _____, also known as property, plant, and equipment (PP&E), is a term used in accountancy for assets and property which cannot easily be converted into cash. This can be compared with current assets such as cash or bank accounts, which are described as liquid assets. In most cases, only tangible assets are referred to as fixed.
   a. Minority interest
   b. Subledger
   c. Bankruptcy prediction
   d. Fixed Asset

22. The Exxon Mobil Corporation is an American oil and gas corporation. It is a direct descendant of John D. Rockefeller's Standard Oil company, formed on November 30, 1999, by the merger of Exxon and Mobil.

_____ is the world's largest publicly traded company when measured by either revenue or market capitalization.

   a. Alan Greenspan
   b. Arthur Betz Laffer
   c. ExxonMobil
   d. Abby Joseph Cohen

23. An _____ is the buying of one company by another. An _____ may be friendly or hostile. In the former case, the companies cooperate in negotiations; in the latter case, the takeover target is unwilling to be bought or the target's board has no prior knowledge of the offer. _____ usually refers to a purchase of a smaller firm by a larger one. Sometimes, however, a smaller firm will acquire management control of a larger or longer established company and keep its name for the combined entity. This is known as a reverse takeover.
   a. AMEX
   b. AIG
   c. ABC Television Network
   d. Acquisition

Chapter 11. Depreciation, Impairments, and Depletion, 95

24. _____ means the giving out of information, either voluntarily or to be in compliance with legal regulations or workplace rules.

- In Computer security, full _____ means disclosing full information about vulnerabilities.
- In computing, _____ widget
- Journalism, full _____ refers to disclosing the interests of the writer which may bear on the subject being written about, for example, if the writer has worked with an interview subject in the past.

- In law:
  - The law of England and Wales, _____ refers to a process that may form part of legal proceedings, whereby parties inform to other parties the existence of any relevant documents that are, or have been, in their control. This compares with the process known as discovery in the course of legal proceedings in the United States.
  - In U.S. civil procedure (litigation rules for civil cases), _____ is a stage prior to trial. In civil cases, each party must disclose to the opposing party the following: names of witnesses which it may use to support its side, copies of documents (or mere description of these documents) in its control which it may use to support its side, computation of damages claimed, and certain insurance information. _____ is related to, but technically prior to, the discovery stage.
  - In Company law (known as 'corporate law' in the United States), _____ refers to giving out information about public or limited companies or their officers, which might be kept secret if the company was a private company or a partnership.

- In real property transactions, _____ refers to providing to a buyer information known to the seller or broker/agent concerning the condition or other aspects of real property that would affect the property's value or desirability. These rules regarding what information must be disclosed, and whether the information must be disclosed even if a buyer does not ask, vary from one jurisdiction to the next.

a. Disclosure
b. Trailing
c. Tax harmonisation
d. Controlled Foreign Corporations

25. A _____ is a form of partnership similar to a general partnership, except that in addition to one or more general partners (GPs), there are one or more limited partners (_____s.) It is a partnership in which only one partner is required to be a general partner.

The GPs are, in all major respects, in the same legal position as partners in a conventional firm, i.e. they have management control, share the right to use partnership property, share the profits of the firm in predefined proportions, and have joint and several liability for the debts of the partnership.

a. Limited Partnership
b. Dow Jones ' Company
c. Debenture
d. Minority interest

26. A _____ is a type of business entity in which partners (owners) share with each other the profits or losses of the business undertaking in which all have invested. _____s are often favored over corporations for taxation purposes, as the _____ structure does not generally incur a tax on profits before it is distributed to the partners (i.e. there is no dividend tax levied.) However, depending on the _____ structure and the jurisdiction in which it operates, owners of a _____ may be exposed to greater personal liability than they would as shareholders of a corporation.

a. Partnership
b. Corporate governance
c. Resource Conservation and Recovery Act
d. National Information Infrastructure Protection Act

27. _____ are those reserves claimed to have a reasonable certainty (normally at least 90% confidence) of being recoverable under existing economic and political conditions, and using existing technology. Industry specialists refer to this as P90 (i.e. having a 90% certainty of being produced). _____ are also known in the industry as 1P.
   a. BNSF Railway
   b. 3M Company
   c. BMC Software, Inc.
   d. Proved reserves

28. _____ are payments made by a corporation to its shareholder members. It is the portion of corporate profits paid out to stockholders. When a corporation earns a profit or surplus, that money can be put to two uses: it can either be re-invested in the business (called retained earnings), or it can be paid to the shareholders as a dividend.
   a. Dividend yield
   b. Dividend stripping
   c. Dividend payout ratio
   d. Dividends

29. _____ is generally understood in financial circles as the point at which revenue is recognized, typically through a transaction which involves the exchange of an asset, product, or service for cash or its equivalents.

This approach gives the accounting division a strictly objective basis for changing the books. For example, a homeowner may believe that his house has grown in value during a strong market, or fallen in value during a weak market, but until the house is actually sold for a specific price to a specific buyer, the change in value can only be estimated and is considered unrealized.

   a. Merck ' Co., Inc.
   b. Valuation
   c. Total-factor productivity
   d. Realization

30. _____ is a payment of a dividend to stockholders that exceeds the company's retained earnings. Once retained earnings is depleted, capital accounts such as additional paid-in capital are decreased to make up for the remaining dividend to be paid to stockholders. When a _____ occurs, it is considered to be a return of investment instead of profits.
   a. Trade name
   b. Liquidating dividend
   c. Fund accounting
   d. Redemption value

31. _____ is any physical or virtual entity that is owned by an individual or jointly by a group of individuals. An owner of _____ has the right to consume, sell, rent, mortgage, transfer and exchange his or her _____. Important widely-recognized types of _____ include real _____, personal _____ (other physical possessions), and intellectual _____ (rights over artistic creations, inventions, etc.), although the latter is not always as widely recognized or enforced.
   a. Fiduciary
   b. Disclosure requirement
   c. Primary authority
   d. Property

32. _____ is a financial ratio that measures the efficiency of a company's use of its assets in generating sales revenue or sales income to the company.

$$Asset\ Turnover = \frac{Sales}{Average\ Total\ Assets}$$

- 'Sales' is the value of 'Net Sales' or 'Sales' from the company's income statement
- 'Average Total Assets' is the value of 'Total assets' from the company's balance sheet in the beginning and the end of the fiscal period divided by 2.

a. Enterprise Value/Sales
c. Asset turnover

b. Average propensity to consume
d. Information ratio

33. _____, net margin, net _____ or net profit ratio all refer to a measure of profitability. It is calculated by finding the net profit as a percentage of the revenue.

$$Net\ profit\ margin = \frac{Net\ profit\ (after\ taxes)}{Revenue} \times 100$$

The _____ is mostly used for internal comparison.

a. BNSF Railway
c. 3M Company

b. BMC Software, Inc.
d. Profit margin

34. In finance, _____ also known as return on investment, rate of profit or sometimes just return, is the ratio of money gained or lost on an investment relative to the amount of money invested. The amount of money gained or lost may be referred to as interest, profit/loss, gain/loss, or net income/loss. The money invested may be referred to as the asset, capital, principal, or the cost basis of the investment.

a. Capital employed
c. Debt to capital ratio

b. Theoretical ex-rights price
d. Rate of return

35. The _____ percentage shows how profitable a company's assets are in generating revenue.

_____ can be computed as:

$$ROA = \frac{Net\ Income - Interest\ Expense - Interest\ Tax\ savings}{Average\ Total\ Assets}$$

This number tells you what the company can do with what it has, i.e. how many dollars of earnings they derive from each dollar of assets they control. Its a useful number for comparing competing companies in the same industry.

a. Return on assets
c. Capital employed

b. Return on sales
d. Statutory Liquidity Ratio

Chapter 11. Depreciation, Impairments, and Depletion,

36. A _____ is the pinnacle activity involved in selling products or services in return for money or other compensation. It is an act of completion of a commercial activity.

A _____ is completed by the seller, the owner of the goods.

   a. Maturity
   b. High yield stock
   c. Tertiary sector of economy
   d. Sale

37. In physics, and more specifically kinematics, _____ is the change in velocity over time. Because velocity is a vector, it can change in two ways: a change in magnitude and/or a change in direction. In one dimension, _____ is the rate at which something speeds up or slows down.
   a. AMEX
   b. Acceleration
   c. ABC Television Network
   d. AIG

38. The _____ is the current method of accelerated asset depreciation required by the United States income tax code. Under _____, all assets are divided into classes which dictate the number of years over which an asset's cost will be recovered.

Prior to the Accelerated Cost Recovery System (ACRS), most capital purchases were depreciated using a straight line technique, that allowed for the depreciation of the asset over its useful life.

   a. Categorical grants
   b. BMC Software, Inc.
   c. Modified Accelerated Cost Recovery System
   d. 3M Company

39. The _____ was 'A bill to amend the Internal Revenue Code of 1954 to encourage economic growth through reductions in individual income tax rates, the expensing of depreciable property, incentives for small businesses, and incentives for savings, and for other purpose.' Pub.L. 97-34, 95 Stat. 172, enacted August 13, 1981) It also reduced marginal income tax rates in the United States by 25% over three years and indexed the rates for inflation, though the indexing was delayed until 1985.
   a. AMEX
   b. ABC Television Network
   c. Economic Recovery Tax Act of 1981
   d. AIG

40. _____ is a company's financial statement that indicates how the revenue is transformed into the net income The purpose of the _____ is to show managers and investors whether the company made or lost money during the period being reported.

The important thing to remember about an _____ is that it represents a period of time.

   a. AIG
   b. Income statement
   c. ABC Television Network
   d. AMEX

41. The _____, increased carryback of net operating losses to 5 years (through September 2003), extended the exception under Subpart F for active financing income (through 2006), and created 30 percent expensing for certain capital asset purchases (through September 2004.)

Chapter 11. Depreciation, Impairments, and Depletion,

a. 3M Company
c. BNSF Railway
b. BMC Software, Inc.
d. Job Creation and Worker Assistance Act of 2002

42. _____ is the process of changing the way taxes are collected or managed by the government.

_____ers have different goals. Some seek to reduce the level of taxation of all people by the government.

a. Tax exporting
c. Tax investigation
b. Franchise tax
d. Tax Reform

43. The U.S. Congress passed the _____, (Pub.L. 99-514, 100 Stat. 2085, enacted October 22, 1986) to simplify the income tax code, broaden the tax base and eliminate many tax shelters and other preferences.

The tax reform was designed to be revenue neutral, but because individual taxes were decreased while corporate taxes were increased, Congressional Budget Office estimates (which ignore corporate taxes) suggested every tax payer saw a decrease in their tax bill. As of 2009, the _____ was the most recent major simplification of the tax code, drastically reducing the number of deductions and the number of tax brackets.

a. BMC Software, Inc.
c. BNSF Railway
b. 3M Company
d. Tax Reform Act of 1986

44. Procter is a surname, and may also refer to:

- Bryan Waller Procter (pseud. Barry Cornwall), English poet
- Goodwin Procter, American law firm
- _____, consumer products multinational

a. Welfare
c. Markup
b. Screening
d. Procter ' Gamble

Chapter 12. Intangible Assets,

1. _____ are defined as identifiable non-monetary assets that cannot be seen, touched or physically measured, which are created through time and/or effort and that are identifiable as a separate asset. There are two primary forms of intangibles - legal intangibles (such as trade secrets (e.g., customer lists), copyrights, patents, trademarks, and goodwill) and competitive intangibles (such as knowledge activities (know-how, knowledge), collaboration activities, leverage activities, and structural activities.) Legal intangibles are known under the generic term intellectual property and generate legal property rights defensible in a court of law.

   a. ABC Television Network
   b. Overhead
   c. AIG
   d. Intangible assets

2. In business and accounting, _____ are everything of value that is owned by a person or company. It is a claim on the property your income of a borrower. The balance sheet of a firm records the monetary value of the _____ owned by the firm.

   a. Accrual basis accounting
   b. Accounts receivable
   c. Assets
   d. Earnings before interest, taxes, depreciation and amortization

3. _____ is the process of increasing, or accounting for, an amount over a period of time. Particular instances of the term include:

   - _____, the allocation of a lump sum amount to different time periods, particularly for loans and other forms of finance, including related interest or other finance charges.
     - _____ schedule, a table detailing each periodic payment on a loan (typically a mortgage), as generated by an _____ calculator.
     - Negative _____, an _____ schedule where the loan amount actually increases through not paying the full interest
   - Amortized analysis, analyzing the execution cost of algorithms over a sequence of operations.
   - _____ of capital expenditures of certain assets under accounting rules, particularly intangible assets, in a manner analogous to depreciation.
   - _____

   a. Annuity
   b. EBIT
   c. Intangible
   d. Amortization

4. In finance, a _____ is a debt security, in which the authorized issuer owes the holders a debt and, depending on the terms of the _____, is obliged to pay interest (the coupon) and/or to repay the principal at a later date, termed maturity. It is a formal contract to repay borrowed money with interest at fixed intervals.

   Thus a _____ is like a loan: the issuer is the borrower, the _____ holder is the lender, and the coupon is the interest.

   a. Zero-coupon bond
   b. Revenue bonds
   c. Coupon rate
   d. Bond

Chapter 12. Intangible Assets, 101

5. In finance, _____ is the process of estimating the potential market value of a financial asset or liability. They can be done on assets (for example, investments in marketable securities such as stocks, options, business enterprises, or intangible assets such as patents and trademarks) or on liabilities (e.g., Bonds issued by a company.) A _____ is required in many contexts including investment analysis, capital budgeting, merger and acquisition transactions, financial reporting, taxable events to determine the proper tax liability, and in litigation.
   a. Daybook
   b. Vyborg Appeal
   c. Disclosure
   d. Valuation

6. A _____ or trade mark, identified by the symbols â„¢ (not yet registered) and Â® (registered), is a distinctive sign or indicator used by an individual, business organization or other legal entity to identify that the products and/or services to consumers with which the _____ appears originate from a unique source, and to distinguish its products or services from those of other entities. A _____ is a type of intellectual property, and typically a name, word, phrase, logo, symbol, design, image, or a combination of these elements. There is also a range of non-conventional _____s comprising marks which do not fall into these standard categories.
   a. Trademark
   b. FIFO
   c. Kanban
   d. Risk management

7. A _____ is the name which a business trades under for commercial purposes, although its registered, legal name, used for contracts and other formal situations, may be another. Pharmaceuticals also have _____s, often dissimilar to their chemical names

Trading names are sometimes registered as trademarks or are regarded as brands.

   a. Fund accounting
   b. Price variance
   c. Trade name
   d. Consumer-to-business

8. _____, also known as Merck Sharp ' Dohme or MSD outside the USA and Canada, is one of the largest pharmaceutical companies in the world. The headquarters of the company is located in Whitehouse Station, New Jersey, an unincorporated area in Readington Township.
   a. Pension System
   b. Social Security
   c. Procter ' Gamble
   d. Merck ' Co., Inc.

9. A _____ is a set of exclusive rights granted by a state to an inventor or his assignee for a limited period of time in exchange for a disclosure of an invention.

The procedure for granting _____s, the requirements placed on the _____ee and the extent of the exclusive rights vary widely between countries according to national laws and international agreements. Typically, however, a _____ application must include one or more claims defining the invention which must be new, inventive, and useful or industrially applicable.

   a. Patent
   b. FLSA
   c. Negligence
   d. Trust indenture

10. The _____ is currently the source of generally accepted accounting principles (GAAP) used by State and Local governments in the [[United States of America]]. As with most of the entities involved in creating GAAP in the United States, it is a private, non-governmental organization.

The _____ is subject to oversight by the Financial Accounting Foundation (FAF), which selects the members of the _____ and the Financial Accounting Standards Board, and funds both organizations.

a. Multinational corporation

b. Fannie Mae

c. Governmental Accounting Standards Board

d. National Conference of Commissioners on Uniform State Laws

11. The term _____ describes a reduction in recognized value. In accounting terminology, it refers to recognition of the reduced or zero value of an asset. In income tax statements, it refers to a reduction of taxable income as recognition of certain expenses required to produce the income.

a. Salvage value

b. Payroll

c. Current asset

d. Write-off

12. _____, also called fair price (in a commonplace conflation of the two distinct concepts), is a concept used in finance and economics, defined as a rational and unbiased estimate of the potential market price of a good, service, or asset, taking into account such objective factors as:

- acquisition/production/distribution costs, replacement costs, or costs of close substitutes
- actual utility at a given level of development of social productive capability
- supply vs. demand

and subjective factors such as

- risk characteristics
- cost of capital
- individually perceived utility

In accounting, _____ is used as an estimate of the market value of an asset (or liability) for which a market price cannot be determined (usually because there is no established market for the asset.) Under GAAP (FAS 157), _____ is the amount at which the asset could be bought or sold in a current transaction between willing parties, or transferred to an equivalent party, other than in a liquidation sale. This is used for assets whose carrying value is based on mark-to-market valuations; for assets carried at historical cost, the _____ of the asset is not used. One example of where _____ is an issue is a College kitchen with a cost of $2 million which was built 5 years ago.

a. BMC Software, Inc.

b. BNSF Railway

c. 3M Company

d. Fair value

13. _____ (NYSE: DE) is an American corporation based in Moline, Illinois, and the leading manufacturer of agricultural machinery in the world. In 2008, it was listed as 102nd in the Fortune 500 ranking. Deere and Company agricultural products, usually sold under the John Deere name, include tractors, combine harvesters, balers, planters/seeders, ATVs and forestry equipment.

Chapter 12. Intangible Assets,

a. Governmental Accounting Standards Board
c. Freddie Mac
b. Professional association
d. Deere ' Company

14. In economics, business, retail, and accounting, a _____ is the value of money that has been used up to produce something, and hence is not available for use anymore. In economics, a _____ is an alternative that is given up as a result of a decision. In business, the _____ may be one of acquisition, in which case the amount of money expended to acquire it is counted as _____.

a. Cost allocation
c. Prime cost
b. Cost of quality
d. Cost

15. The _____ founded on April 1, 2001 is the successor of the International Accounting Standards Committee (IASC) founded in June 1973 in London. It is responsible for developing the International Financial Reporting Standards (new name for the International Accounting Standards issued after 2001), and promoting the use and application of these standards.

The _____ is an independent, privately-funded accounting standard-setter based in London, UK.

a. Institute of Management Accountants
c. Information Systems Audit and Control Association
b. International Accounting Standards Board
d. Emerging technologies

16. Procter is a surname, and may also refer to:

- Bryan Waller Procter (pseud. Barry Cornwall), English poet
- Goodwin Procter, American law firm
- _____, consumer products multinational

a. Welfare
c. Markup
b. Procter ' Gamble
d. Screening

Chapter 13. Current Liabilities and Contingencies,

1. _____ is the term used to refer to the standard framework of guidelines for financial accounting used in any given jurisdiction. _____ includes the standards, conventions, and rules accountants follow in recording and summarizing transactions, and in the preparation of financial statements.

Financial accounting information must be assembled and reported objectively.

a. Long-term liabilities
b. Current asset
c. General ledger
d. Generally accepted accounting principles

2. _____s are cash, evidence of an ownership interest in an entity or deliver, cash or another _____.

_____s can be categorized by form depending on whether they are cash instruments or derivative instruments:

- Cash instruments are _____s whose value is determined directly by markets. They can be divided into securities, which are readily transferable, and other cash instruments such as loans and deposits, where both borrower and lender have to agree on a transfer.
- Derivative instruments are _____s which derive their value from the value and characteristics of one or more underlying assets. They can be divided into exchange-traded derivatives and over-the-counter (OTC) derivatives.

Alternatively, _____s can be categorized by 'asset class' depending on whether they are equity based (reflecting ownership of the issuing entity) or debt based (reflecting a loan the investor has made to the issuing entity.) If it is debt, it can be further categorised into short term (less than one year) or long term.

Foreign Exchange instruments and transactions are neither debt nor equity based and belong in their own category.

a. Market price
b. Financial instruments
c. Mark-to-market
d. Financial Instrument

3. _____ are cash, evidence of an ownership interest in an entity, or a contractual right to receive, or deliver, cash or another financial instrument.

_____ can be categorized by form depending on whether they are cash instruments or derivative instruments:

- Cash instruments are _____ whose value is determined directly by markets. They can be divided into securities, which are readily transferable, and other cash instruments such as loans and deposits, where both borrower and lender have to agree on a transfer.
- Derivative instruments are _____ which derive their value from the value and characteristics of one or more underlying assets. They can be divided into exchange-traded derivatives and over-the-counter (OTC) derivatives.

Alternatively, _____ can be categorized by 'asset class' depending on whether they are equity based (reflecting ownership of the issuing entity) or debt based (reflecting a loan the investor has made to the issuing entity.) If it is debt, it can be further categorised into short term (less than one year) or long term.

Foreign Exchange instruments and transactions are neither debt nor equity based and belong in their own category.

   a. Financial Instruments
   b. Market liquidity
   c. Transfer agent
   d. Spot rate

4. In financial accounting, a _____ is defined as an obligation of an entity arising from past transactions or events, the settlement of which may result in the transfer or use of assets, provision of services or other yielding of economic benefits in the future.

   a. Vested
   b. Liability
   c. Corporate governance
   d. False Claims Act

5. _____ is a file or account that contains money that a person or company owes to suppliers, but has not paid yet (a form of debt.) When you receive an invoice you add it to the file, and then you remove it when you pay. Thus, the A/P is a form of credit that suppliers offer to their purchasers by allowing them to pay for a product or service after it has already been received.

   a. Accrual
   b. Accounts receivable
   c. Earnings before interest, taxes, depreciation and amortization
   d. Accounts payable

6. In accounting, _____ are considered liabilities of the business that are to be settled in cash within the fiscal year or the operating cycle, whichever period is longer.

For example accounts payable for goods, services or supplies that were purchased for use in the operation of the business and payable within a normal period of time would be _____.

Bonds, mortgages and loans that are payable over a term exceeding one year would be fixed liabilities.

   a. Payroll
   b. Closing entries
   c. Treasury stock
   d. Current liabilities

7. _____ are formal records of a business' financial activities.

In British English, including United Kingdom company law, _____ are often referred to as accounts, although the term _____ is also used, particularly by accountants.

_____ provide an overview of a business' financial condition in both short and long term.

Chapter 13. Current Liabilities and Contingencies,

a. Financial Statements
b. Statement of retained earnings
c. 3M Company
d. Notes to the financial statements

8. In economics, the concept of the _____ refers to the decision-making time frame of a firm in which at least one factor of production is fixed. Costs which are fixed in the _____ have no impact on a firms decisions. For example a firm can raise output by increasing the amount of labour through overtime.
   a. Long-run
   b. Short-run
   c. 3M Company
   d. BMC Software, Inc.

9. A _____, also referred to as a note payable in accounting, is a contract where one party (the maker or issuer) makes an unconditional promise in writing to pay a sum of money to the other (the payee), either at a fixed or determinable future time or on demand of the payee, under specific terms. They differ from IOUs in that they contain a specific promise to pay, rather than simply acknowledging that a debt exists.

The terms of a note typically include the principal amount, the interest rate if any, and the maturity date.

   a. BMC Software, Inc.
   b. 3M Company
   c. BNSF Railway
   d. Promissory note

10. In economic models, the _____ time frame assumes no fixed factors of production. Firms can enter or leave the marketplace, and the cost (and availability) of land, labor, raw materials, and capital goods can be assumed to vary. In contrast, in the short-run time frame, certain factors are assumed to be fixed, because there is not sufficient time for them to change.
    a. BMC Software, Inc.
    b. Short-run
    c. 3M Company
    d. Long-run

11. _____ is that which is owed; usually referencing assets owed, but the term can also cover moral obligations and other interactions not requiring money. In the case of assets, _____ is a means of using future purchasing power in the present before a summation has been earned. Some companies and corporations use _____ as a part of their overall corporate finance strategy.
    a. Debenture
    b. Debt
    c. Lender
    d. Loan

12. A _____ is a type of bond that allows the issuer of the bond to retain the privilege of redeeming the bond at some point before the bond reaches the date of maturity. In other words, on the call dates, the issuer has the right, but not the obligation, to buy back the bonds from the bond holders at the call price. Technically speaking, the bonds are not really bought and held by the issuer but cancelled immediately.
    a. Callable bond
    b. Catastrophe bonds
    c. Coupon rate
    d. Zero-coupon

13. A _____ is a party (e.g. person, organization, company, or government) that has a claim to the services of a second party. It is a person or institution to whom money is owed. The first party, in general, has provided some property or service to the second party under the assumption (usually enforced by contract) that the second party will return an equivalent property or service.

a. Payback period
b. Treasury company
c. Par value
d. Creditor

14. _____ refers to the replacement of an existing debt obligation with a debt obligation bearing different terms. The most common consumer _____ is for a home mortgage.

_____ may be undertaken to reduce interest rate/interest costs (by _____ at a lower rate), to extend the repayment time, to pay off other debt(s), to reduce one's periodic payment obligations (sometimes by taking a longer-term loan), to reduce or alter risk (such as by _____ from a variable-rate to a fixed-rate loan), and/or to raise cash for investment, consumption, or the payment of a dividend.

a. BMC Software, Inc.
b. BNSF Railway
c. 3M Company
d. Refinancing

15. In economics, _____ or _____ goods or real _____ refers to factors of production used to create goods or services that are not themselves significantly consumed (though they may depreciate) in the production process. _____ goods may be acquired with money or financial _____. In finance and accounting, _____ generally refers to financial wealth, especially that used to start or maintain a business.
a. Disclosure
b. Screening
c. Vyborg Appeal
d. Capital

16. _____ are payments made by a corporation to its shareholder members. It is the portion of corporate profits paid out to stockholders. When a corporation earns a profit or surplus, that money can be put to two uses: it can either be re-invested in the business (called retained earnings), or it can be paid to the shareholders as a dividend.
a. Dividend stripping
b. Dividends
c. Dividend payout ratio
d. Dividend yield

17. _____, in accrual accounting, (e.g. advance payment received from a client) is, according to revenue recognition, revenue not earned until the delivery of goods or services, which until then, is still owed to the payer, hence remaining a liability.

_____, sometimes referred to as deferred revenue or unearned revenue, shares characteristics with accrued expense with the difference that a liability to be covered latter is cash received FROM a counterpart, while goods or services are to be delivered in a latter period, when such income item is earned, the related revenue item is recognized, and the same amount is deducted from deferred revenues.

a. Matching principle
b. Treasury stock
c. Gross sales
d. Deferred income

18. _____ is a legal term for a type of debt which is overdue after missing an expected payment. It is also used (in the form in _____) for payments that occur at the end of a period.

_____ accrue from the date on the first missed payment was due. The term is often used to describe being late with rent, bills, royalties (or other contractual payments), child support, or other legal financial obligation.

a. AIG
b. Arrears
c. Interest
d. ABC Television Network

19. A _____ is the pinnacle activity involved in selling products or services in return for money or other compensation. It is an act of completion of a commercial activity.

A _____ is completed by the seller, the owner of the goods.

a. Maturity
b. Tertiary sector of economy
c. Sale
d. High yield stock

20. _____ refers to a tax levied by various jurisdictions on the profits made by companies or associations. It is a tax on the value of the corporation's profits.

The measure of taxable profits varies from country to country.

a. Transfer tax
b. Rational economic exchange
c. Corporate tax
d. Tax protester

21. An _____ is a tax levied on the financial income of people, corporations, or other legal entities. Various _____ systems exist, with varying degrees of tax incidence. Income taxation can be progressive, proportional, or regressive.

a. Income tax
b. Implied level of government service
c. Ordinary income
d. Individual Retirement Arrangement

22. The _____ is a private, not-for-profit organization whose primary purpose is to develop generally accepted accounting principles (GAAP) within the United States in the public's interest. The Securities and Exchange Commission (SEC) designated the _____ as the organization responsible for setting accounting standards for public companies in the U.S. It was created in 1973, replacing the Accounting Principles Board and the Committee on Accounting Procedure of the American Institute of Certified Public Accountants. The _____'s mission is 'to establish and improve standards of financial accounting and reporting for the guidance and education of the public, including issuers, auditors, and users of financial information.'

The _____ is not a governmental body.

a. Financial Accounting Standards Board
b. Public company
c. Fannie Mae
d. Governmental Accounting Standards Board

23. The _____ is a United States federal law that imposes a federal employer tax used to fund state workforce agencies. Employers report this tax by filing an annual Form 940 with the Internal Revenue Service.

a. Federal Unemployment Tax Act
b. Transfer tax
c. Council Tax
d. Tax evasion

Chapter 13. Current Liabilities and Contingencies,

24. _____, in law and economics, is a form of risk management primarily used to hedge against the risk of a contingent loss. _____ is defined as the equitable transfer of the risk of a loss, from one entity to another, in exchange for a premium, and can be thought of as a guaranteed small loss to prevent a large, possibly devastating loss. An insurer is a company selling the _____; an insured is the person or entity buying the _____.

a. AIG
b. ABC Television Network
c. AMEX
d. Insurance

25. In a company, _____ is the sum of all financial records of salaries, wages, bonuses and deductions.

A paycheck, is traditionally a paper document issued by an employer to pay an employee for services rendered. While most commonly used in the United States, recently the physical paycheck has been increasingly replaced by electronic direct deposit to bank accounts.

a. 3M Company
b. Tax expense
c. Total Expense Ratio
d. Payroll

26. A _____ is a fungible, negotiable instrument representing financial value. they are broadly categorized into debt securities (such as banknotes, bonds and debentures), and equity securities; e.g., common stocks. The company or other entity issuing the _____ is called the issuer.

a. Security
b. BMC Software, Inc.
c. Tracking stock
d. 3M Company

27. _____ in the United States currently refers to the federal Old-Age, Survivors, and Disability Insurance (OASDI) program.

The original _____ Act and the current version of the Act, as amended encompass several social welfare and social insurance programs. The larger and better known programs are:

- Federal Old-Age, Survivors, and Disability Insurance
- Unemployment benefits
- Temporary Assistance for Needy Families
- Health Insurance for Aged and Disabled (Medicare)
- Grants to States for Medical Assistance Programs (Medicaid)
- State Children's Health Insurance Program (SCHIP)
- Supplemental Security Income (Social Securityl)

U.S. _____ is a social insurance program funded through dedicated payroll taxes called Federal Insurance Contributions Act (FICA.) Tax deposits are formally entrusted to Federal Old-Age and Survivors Insurance Trust Fund, or Federal Disability Insurance Trust Fund, Federal Hospital Insurance Trust Fund or the Federal Supplementary Medical Insurance Trust Fund.

a. Social Security
b. Sale
c. Comparable
d. Price-to-sales ratio

Chapter 13. Current Liabilities and Contingencies,

28. Employment is a contract between two parties, one being the employer and the other being the _____. An _____ may be defined as: 'A person in the service of another under any contract of hire, express or implied, oral or written, where the employer has the power or right to control and direct the _____ in the material details of how the work is to be performed.' Black's Law Dictionary page 471 (5th ed. 1979.)
   a. ABC Television Network   b. AMEX
   c. Employee   d. AIG

29. _____ methods are means of managing inventory and financial matters involving the money a company ties up within inventory of produced goods, raw materials, parts, components, or feed stocks. FIFO stands for first-in, first-out, meaning that the oldest inventory items are recorded as sold first. LIFO stands for last-in, first-out, meaning that the most recently purchased items are recorded as sold first.
   a. FIFO and LIFO accounting   b. 3M Company
   c. Reorder point   d. Finished good

30. _____ generally refers to two kinds of taxes: Taxes which employers are required to withhold from employees' pay Pay-As-You-Earn or Pay-As-You-Go tax; and taxes which are paid from the employer's own funds and which are directly related to employing a worker, which may be either fixed charges or proportionally linked to an employee's pay.

In Australia, the _____ is a specific tax which is paid to states and territories by employers, not by employees. The tax is not deducted from the worker's pay.

   a. Payroll tax   b. Nonbusiness Energy Property Tax Credit
   c. Federal Unemployment Tax Act   d. Passive foreign investment company

31. In law, vesting is to give an immediately secured right of present or future enjoyment. One has a _____ right to an asset that cannot be taken away by any third party, even though one may not yet possess the asset. When the right, interest or title to the present or future possession of a legal estate can be transferred to any other party, it is termed a _____ interest.
   a. Malpractice   b. Liability
   c. Vested   d. Tax lien

32. In accounting, _____ has a very specific meaning. It is an outflow of cash or other valuable assets from a person or company to another person or company. This outflow of cash is generally one side of a trade for products or services that have equal or better current or future value to the buyer than to the seller.
   a. ABC Television Network   b. AMEX
   c. AIG   d. Expense

33. _____, also known as Merck Sharp ' Dohme or MSD outside the USA and Canada, is one of the largest pharmaceutical companies in the world. The headquarters of the company is located in Whitehouse Station, New Jersey, an unincorporated area in Readington Township.
   a. Social Security   b. Procter ' Gamble
   c. Pension System   d. Merck ' Co., Inc.

Chapter 13. Current Liabilities and Contingencies,

34. Briggs could refer to:

- Briggs cliff, a fictional place in Fullmetal Alchemist manga
- Briggs (crater), a lunar crater
- Briggs Initiative, either of two pieces of Californian legislation sponsored by John Briggs
- Briggs Islet, Tasmania, Australia
- Briggs, Oklahoma, USA
- Briggs, Texas, USA
- _____, a manufacturer of air-cooled gasoline engines
- The Briggs - a punk rock band
- Myers-Briggs Type Indicator

- Anne Briggs, English folk singer
- Ansel Briggs, American politician
- Arthur E. Briggs, California politician
- Asa Briggs, British historian
- Barbara Briggs, American dramatist
- Barbara G. Briggs, Australian botanist
- Barry Briggs, New Zealand World Motorcycle speedway champion
- Barry Bruce-Briggs, public policy writer
- Benjamin Briggs, captain of the Mary Celeste
- Bill Briggs, American skier
- Billy Briggs, American musician
- Bobby Briggs, fictional character from Twin Peaks
- Charles Augustus Briggs, American theologian
- Charles Frederick Briggs, American journalist
- Clare Briggs, American comics artist
- David Briggs:
    - David Briggs (producer) (1944-1995), American record producer
    - David Briggs (composer) English organist and composer
    - David Briggs (Australian musician) , guitarist with Little River Band and Australian record producer
- Derek Briggs, Irish paleontologist
- Everett Francis Briggs, (1908-2006), American Catholic priest
- Frank A. Briggs, American politician
- Frank O. Briggs, American politician
- Frank P. Briggs, American politician
- Gary Briggs (musician), British guitarist
- Gary Briggs (footballer), British footballer
- George N. Briggs, American politician
- Major Garland Briggs, fictional character from Twin Peaks
- Harold Briggs
    - Harold Briggs (General), British general
    - Harold Briggs (politician), British Conservative MP
- Henry Briggs (politician)
- Henry Briggs (mathematician), English mathematician
- Hortense Briggs, fictional character from An American Tragedy by Theodore Dreiser
- Ian Briggs, television writer
- Jack Briggs, American instrument maker
- James Briggs, any of several people
- Jason W. Briggs, American Latter Day Saint leader
- Jeff Briggs, American computer games executive
- Joe Bob Briggs, pseudonym of John Irving Bloom, film critic and actor
- John Briggs (politician), a California politician
- John Briggs (author)
- Johnny Briggs:

- - Johnny Briggs (cricketer)
  - Johnny Briggs (actor), actor who played Mike Baldwin on the British soap opera Coronation Street
  - Johnny Briggs (baseball), a former Major League Baseball outfielder
- Jon Briggs, British radio personality
- Jonny Briggs, BBC children's television programme first broadcast in 1985.
- Karen Briggs, American violinist
- Katharine Cook Briggs, co-inventor of the Myers-Briggs Type Indicator personality test
- Katharine Mary Briggs, British author
- Kevin 'She'kspere' Briggs, American record producer
- Lance Briggs, American football player
- LeBaron Russell Briggs, American educator
- Lyman James Briggs, American physicist and civil servant
- Matilda Briggs, passenger on the Marie Celeste
- Matthew Briggs, English footballer
- Nicholas Briggs, British actor
- Nigel Briggs, Singer/Song writer
- Patricia Briggs, American fantasy writer
- Paul Briggs, Australian boxer
- Raymond Briggs, British illustrator and author
- Sandra Briggs, fictional character from Emmerdale
- Shannon Briggs, American boxer
- Stephen Briggs, British Discworld adapter
- Stephen Foster Briggs, American engineer, co-founder of The _____ Company
- Ted Briggs, British seaman
- Tom Briggs, American football player
- Walter Briggs, Major League Baseball owner

a. Briggs ' Stratton
b. BMC Software, Inc.
c. 3M Company
d. BNSF Railway

35. The _____ is the former authoritative body of the American Institute of Certified Public Accountants (AICPA.) It was created by the American Institute of Certified Public Accountants in 1959 and issued pronouncements on accounting principles until 1973, when it was replaced by the Financial Accounting Standards Board (FASB.)

The _____ was disbanded in the hopes that the smaller, fully-independent FASB could more effectively create accounting standards.

a. Institute of Management Accountants
b. International Federation of Accountants
c. American Payroll Association
d. Accounting Principles Board

36. _____ of something is, in finance, the adding together of interest or different investments over a period of time such as atoms (1 - the act or process of accruing; 2 - the amount that accrues.) It holds specific meanings in accounting and payroll.

_____, in accounting, describes the accounting method known as _____ basis, whereby revenues and expenses are recognized when they are accrued, i.e. accumulated (earned or incurred), regardless when the actual cash is received or paid out.

a. Accounts receivable
b. Earnings before interest, taxes, depreciation and amortization
c. Assets
d. Accrual

37. _____ is a method of accounting whereby economic activities (rather than cash flow) of financial events are considered, because of two complementary principles, which (together) determine the point, at which expenses and revenues are recognized. According to revenue recognition principle, revenues are realized when earned, whether or not they are received in cash.

a. Earnings before interest, taxes, depreciation and amortization
b. Accrued revenue
c. Accrual
d. Accrual basis accounting

38. _____ is a method of accounting whereby cash flow of financial events is considered. The method recognizes revenues when cash is received and recognizes expenses when cash is paid out. In cash accounting, revenues and expenses are also called cash receipts and cash payments respectively.

a. Closing entries
b. Cash basis accounting
c. Net sales
d. Treasury stock

39. An _____ is quite usually a standard guarantee from the seller of a product that specifies the extent to which the quality or performance of the product is assured and states the conditions under which the product can be returned, replaced, or repaired. It is often given in the form of a specific, written 'Warranty' document. However, a warranty may also arise by operation of law based upon the seller's description of the goods, and perhaps their source and quality, and any material deviation from that specification would violate the guarantee.

a. Exclusive right
b. Escheat
c. Operating Lease
d. Express warranty

40. In economics, business, retail, and accounting, a _____ is the value of money that has been used up to produce something, and hence is not available for use anymore. In economics, a _____ is an alternative that is given up as a result of a decision. In business, the _____ may be one of acquisition, in which case the amount of money expended to acquire it is counted as _____.
   a. Cost allocation
   b. Cost
   c. Prime cost
   d. Cost of quality

41. In marketing a _____ is a ticket or document that can be exchanged for a financial discount or rebate when purchasing a product. Customarily, _____s are issued by manufacturers of consumer packaged goods or by retailers, to be used in retail stores as a part of sales promotions. They are often widely distributed through mail, magazines, newspapers, the Internet, and mobile devices such as cell phones.
   a. BMC Software, Inc.
   b. Merchandising
   c. 3M Company
   d. Coupon

42. _____ means the giving out of information, either voluntarily or to be in compliance with legal regulations or workplace rules.

   - In Computer security, full _____ means disclosing full information about vulnerabilities.
   - In computing, _____ widget
   - Journalism, full _____ refers to disclosing the interests of the writer which may bear on the subject being written about, for example, if the writer has worked with an interview subject in the past.

   - In law:
     - The law of England and Wales, _____ refers to a process that may form part of legal proceedings, whereby parties inform to other parties the existence of any relevant documents that are, or have been, in their control. This compares with the process known as discovery in the course of legal proceedings in the United States.
     - In U.S. civil procedure (litigation rules for civil cases), _____ is a stage prior to trial. In civil cases, each party must disclose to the opposing party the following: names of witnesses which it may use to support its side, copies of documents (or mere description of these documents) in its control which it may use to support its side, computation of damages claimed, and certain insurance information. _____ is related to, but technically prior to, the discovery stage.
     - In Company law (known as 'corporate law' in the United States), _____ refers to giving out information about public or limited companies or their officers, which might be kept secret if the company was a private company or a partnership.

   - In real property transactions, _____ refers to providing to a buyer information known to the seller or broker/agent concerning the condition or other aspects of real property that would affect the property's value or desirability. These rules regarding what information must be disclosed, and whether the information must be disclosed even if a buyer does not ask, vary from one jurisdiction to the next.

Chapter 13. Current Liabilities and Contingencies,

a. Tax harmonisation
c. Trailing
b. Controlled Foreign Corporations
d. Disclosure

43. Most patent law systems require that a patent application disclose a claimed invention in sufficient detail for the notional person skilled in the art to carry out that claimed invention. This requirement is often known as sufficiency of disclosure or enablement, depending on the jurisdiction.

The _____ lies at the heart and origin of patent law. A state or government grants an inventor, or the inventor's assignee, a monopoly for a given period of time in exchange for the inventor disclosing to the public how to make or practice his or her invention. If a patent fails to contain such information, then the bargain is violated, and the patent is unenforceable.

a. False Claims Act
c. Tax patent
b. Pre-emption right
d. Disclosure Requirement

44. In business and accounting, _____ are everything of value that is owned by a person or company. It is a claim on the property your income of a borrower. The balance sheet of a firm records the monetary value of the _____ owned by the firm.

a. Accounts receivable
c. Earnings before interest, taxes, depreciation and amortization
b. Accrual basis accounting
d. Assets

45. _____ provide for future disposal of assets as required by SFAS 143 .

Firms must recognize the _____ liability in the period it was acquired, generally acquisition. The liability equals the market value, and if that is not available the present value of cash flows that will be required to extinguish the liability. An asset equal to the initial liability is added to the Balance Sheet, and depreciated over the life of the asset. The result is an increase in both assets and liabilities.

a. AMEX
c. ABC Television Network
b. Asset retirement obligations
d. AIG

46. _____ is the calculated approximation of a result which is usable even if input data may be incomplete or uncertain.

In statistics, see _____ theory, estimator.

In mathematics, approximation or _____ typically means finding upper or lower bounds of a quantity that cannot readily be computed precisely and is also an educated guess .

a. AMEX
c. AIG
b. ABC Television Network
d. Estimation

Chapter 13. Current Liabilities and Contingencies,

47. The U.S. _____ is an independent agency of the United States government which holds primary responsibility for enforcing the federal securities laws and regulating the securities industry, the nation's stock and options exchanges, and other electronic securities markets. The SEC was created by section 4 of the Securities Exchange Act of 1934 (now codified as 15 U.S.C. ÂÂ§ 78d and commonly referred to as the 1934 Act.)

a. 3M Company
b. BNSF Railway
c. BMC Software, Inc.
d. Securities and Exchange Commission

48. The _____ of 2002 (Pub.L. 107-204, 116 Stat. 745, enacted July 30, 2002), also known as the Public Company Accounting Reform and Investor Protection Act of 2002, is a United States federal law enacted on July 30, 2002 in response to a number of major corporate and accounting scandals including those affecting Enron, Tyco International, Adelphia, Peregrine Systems and WorldCom. The legislation establishes new or enhanced standards for all U.S. public company boards, management, and public accounting firms. It does not apply to privately held companies.

a. Sarbanes-Oxley Act
b. Lease
c. Fair Labor Standards Act
d. FCPA

49. _____ is a risk management method in which a calculated amount of money is set aside to compensate for the potential future loss.

If _____ is approached as a serious risk management technique, money is set aside using actuarial and insurance information and the law of large numbers so that the amount set aside (similar to an insurance premium) is enough to cover the future uncertain loss.

_____ is possible for any insurable risk, meaning a risk that is predictable and measurable enough in the aggregate to be able to estimate the amount that needs to be set aside to pay for future uncertain losses.

a. Loss ratio
b. 3M Company
c. BMC Software, Inc.
d. Self insurance

50. _____ is a fee paid on borrowed assets. It is the price paid for the use of borrowed money, or, money earned by deposited funds. Assets that are sometimes lent with _____ include money, shares, consumer goods through hire purchase, major assets such as aircraft, and even entire factories in finance lease arrangements. The _____ is calculated upon the value of the assets in the same manner as upon money.

a. ABC Television Network
b. AIG
c. Insolvency
d. Interest

51. The _____ is a financial ratio that measures whether or not a firm has enough resources to pay its debts over the next 12 months. It compares a firm's current assets to its current liabilities. It is expressed as follows:

$$\text{Current ratio} = \frac{\text{Current Assets}}{\text{Current Liabilities}}$$

For example, if WXY Company's current assets are $50,000,000 and its current liabilities are $40,000,000, then its _____ would be $50,000,000 divided by $40,000,000, which equals 1.25.

a. Current ratio
b. Return on capital
c. Net Interest Income
d. Times interest earned

52. The _____ is currently the source of generally accepted accounting principles (GAAP) used by State and Local governments in the [[United States of America]]. As with most of the entities involved in creating GAAP in the United States, it is a private, non-governmental organization.

The _____ is subject to oversight by the Financial Accounting Foundation (FAF), which selects the members of the _____ and the Financial Accounting Standards Board, and funds both organizations.

a. Governmental Accounting Standards Board
b. Fannie Mae
c. Multinational corporation
d. National Conference of Commissioners on Uniform State Laws

53. _____ is a financial metric which represents operating liquidity available to a business. Along with fixed assets such as plant and equipment, _____ is considered a part of operating capital. It is calculated as current assets minus current liabilities.

a. BMC Software, Inc.
b. 3M Company
c. Working capital management
d. Working capital

54. In finance, the _____ or quick ratio or liquid ratio measures the ability of a company to use its near cash or quick assets to immediately extinguish or retire its current liabilities. Quick assets include those current assets that presumably can be quickly converted to cash at close to their book values.

$$\text{Quick (Acid Test) Ratio} = \frac{\text{Cash + Marketable Securities + Accounts Receivables}}{\text{Current Liabilities}}$$

Generally, the acid test ratio should be 1:1 or better, however this varies widely by industry.

a. Earnings per share
b. Invested capital
c. Inventory turnover
d. Acid-test

55. Procter is a surname, and may also refer to:

- Bryan Waller Procter (pseud. Barry Cornwall), English poet
- Goodwin Procter, American law firm
- _____, consumer products multinational

a. Screening
b. Welfare
c. Markup
d. Procter ' Gamble

Chapter 14. Long-Term Liabilities,

1. _____ was founded in 1898 by Frank Seiberling. Today it is the third largest tire company in the world after Bridgestone and Michelin. Goodyear manufactures tires for automobiles, commercial trucks, light trucks, SUVs, race cars, airplanes, and heavy earth-mover machinery.
   a. Trailing
   b. Fiscal
   c. Factor
   d. The Goodyear Tire ' Rubber Company

2. In economic models, the _____ time frame assumes no fixed factors of production. Firms can enter or leave the marketplace, and the cost (and availability) of land, labor, raw materials, and capital goods can be assumed to vary. In contrast, in the short-run time frame, certain factors are assumed to be fixed, because there is not sufficient time for them to change.
   a. Short-run
   b. 3M Company
   c. BMC Software, Inc.
   d. Long-run

3. _____ are liabilities with a future benefit over one year, such as notes payable that mature greater than one year.

In accounting, the _____ are shown on the right wing of the balance-sheet representing the sources of funds, which are generally bounded in form of capital assets.

Examples of _____ are debentures, mortgage loans and other bank loans (note: not all bank loans are long term as not all are paid over a period greater than a year, the example is bridging loan.)

   a. Gross sales
   b. Long-term liabilities
   c. Cash basis accounting
   d. Book value

4. In financial accounting, a _____ is defined as an obligation of an entity arising from past transactions or events, the settlement of which may result in the transfer or use of assets, provision of services or other yielding of economic benefits in the future.
   a. False Claims Act
   b. Liability
   c. Corporate governance
   d. Vested

5. In finance, a _____ is a debt security, in which the authorized issuer owes the holders a debt and, depending on the terms of the _____, is obliged to pay interest (the coupon) and/or to repay the principal at a later date, termed maturity. It is a formal contract to repay borrowed money with interest at fixed intervals.

Thus a _____ is like a loan: the issuer is the borrower, the _____ holder is the lender, and the coupon is the interest.

   a. Zero-coupon bond
   b. Revenue bonds
   c. Coupon rate
   d. Bond

6. _____ is that which is owed; usually referencing assets owed, but the term can also cover moral obligations and other interactions not requiring money. In the case of assets, _____ is a means of using future purchasing power in the present before a summation has been earned. Some companies and corporations use _____ as a part of their overall corporate finance strategy.
   a. Loan
   b. Debenture
   c. Lender
   d. Debt

Chapter 14. Long-Term Liabilities,

7. _____ are formal records of a business' financial activities.

In British English, including United Kingdom company law, _____ are often referred to as accounts, although the term _____ is also used, particularly by accountants.

_____ provide an overview of a business' financial condition in both short and long term.

   a. Notes to the financial statements
   b. 3M Company
   c. Financial statements
   d. Statement of retained earnings

8. An _____ is a security whose value and income payments are derived from and collateralized (or 'backed') by a specified pool of underlying assets. The pool of assets is typically a group of small and illiquid assets that are unable to be sold individually. Pooling the assets allows them to be sold to general investors, a process called securitization, and allows the risk of investing in the underlying assets to be diversified because each security will represent a fraction of the total value of the diverse pool of underlying assets.
   a. ABC Television Network
   b. AIG
   c. AMEX
   d. Asset-backed security

9. _____ is a legal document issued to lenders and describes key terms such as the interest rate, maturity date, convertibility, pledge, promises, representations, covenants, and other terms of the bond offering. When the Offering Memorandum is prepared in advance of marketing a Bond, the indenture will typically be summarised in the 'Description of Notes' section.
   a. Malpractice
   b. Leasing
   c. Consumer protection laws
   d. Bond indenture

10. A _____ is a type of bond that allows the issuer of the bond to retain the privilege of redeeming the bond at some point before the bond reaches the date of maturity. In other words, on the call dates, the issuer has the right, but not the obligation, to buy back the bonds from the bond holders at the call price. Technically speaking, the bonds are not really bought and held by the issuer but cancelled immediately.
    a. Callable bond
    b. Zero-coupon
    c. Catastrophe bonds
    d. Coupon rate

11. In finance, a _____ is a type of bond that can be converted into shares of stock in the issuing company, usually at some pre-announced ratio. It is a hybrid security with debt- and equity-like features. Although it typically has a low coupon rate, the holder is compensated with the ability to convert the bond to common stock, usually at a substantial discount to the stock's market value.
    a. Zero-coupon bond
    b. Coupon rate
    c. Zero-coupon
    d. Convertible bond

12. A _____ is defined as a certificate of agreement of loans which is given under the company's stamp and carries an undertaking that the _____ holder will get a fixed return (fixed on the basis of interest rates) and the principal amount whenever the _____ matures.

In finance, a _____ is a long-term debt instrument used by governments and large companies to obtain funds. It is defined as 'any form of borrowing that commits a firm to pay interest and repay capital.

a. Credit rating
c. Loan to value
b. Loan
d. Debenture

13. Discounting is a financial mechanism in which a debtor obtains the right to delay payments to a creditor, for a defined period of time, in exchange for a charge or fee. Essentially, the party that owes money in the present purchases the right to delay the payment until some future date. The _____, or charge, is simply the difference between the original amount owed in the present and the amount that has to be paid in the future to settle the debt.
   a. Risk aversion
   c. Discount
   b. Discount factor
   d. Discounting

14. A _____ is a bond bought at a price lower than its face value, with the face value repaid at the time of maturity. It does not make periodic interest payments, or so-called 'coupons,' hence the term _____. Investors earn return from the compounded interest all paid at maturity plus the difference between the discounted price of the bond and its par value.
   a. Premium bond
   c. Municipal bond
   b. Callable bond
   d. Zero-coupon bond

15. _____ are financial bonds that mature in installments over a period of time. In effect, a $100,000, 5-year serial bond would mature in a $20,000 annuity over a 5-year interval. Bond issues consisting of a series of blocks of securities maturing in sequence, the coupon rate can be different.
   a. Low Income Housing Tax Credit
   c. Serial bonds
   b. Household and Dependent Care Credit
   d. Just-in-time

16. An _____ is a legal contract between two parties, particularly for indentured labour or a term of apprenticeship but also for certain land transactions. The term comes from the medieval English '_____ of retainer' -- a legal contract written in duplicate on the same sheet, with the copies separated by cutting along a jagged line so that the teeth of the two parts could later be refitted to confirm authenticity. Each party to the deed would then retain a part.
   a. Employee Retirement Income Security Act
   c. Operating Lease
   b. Impracticability
   d. Indenture

17. A _____ is a debt security issued by a business entity, such as a corporation, or by a government. It differs from the more common types of investment securities in that it is unregistered - no records are kept of the owner, or the transactions involving ownership. Whoever physically holds the paper on which the bond is issued owns the instrument.
   a. Coupon rate
   c. Revenue bonds
   b. Bearer bond
   d. Convertible bond

18. A _____ is a bond issued by a corporation. It is a bond that a corporation issues to raise money in order to expand its business. The term is usually applied to longer-term debt instruments, generally with a maturity date falling at least a year after their issue date.
   a. Corporate bond
   c. Disclosure
   b. Screening
   d. Merck ' Co., Inc.

19. In marketing a _____ is a ticket or document that can be exchanged for a financial discount or rebate when purchasing a product. Customarily, _____s are issued by manufacturers of consumer packaged goods or by retailers, to be used in retail stores as a part of sales promotions. They are often widely distributed through mail, magazines, newspapers, the Internet, and mobile devices such as cell phones.

Chapter 14. Long-Term Liabilities,

a. Merchandising
c. BMC Software, Inc.
b. Coupon
d. 3M Company

20. A _____ is like a lottery bond issued by the United Kingdom government's National Savings and Investments scheme. The government promises to buy back the bond, on request, for its original price.

_____s were introduced by the government in 1956, with the aim of encouraging saving and controlling inflation, with the first bonds going on sale on 1 November of that year.

a. Callable bond
c. Revenue bonds
b. Premium bond
d. Zero-coupon bond

21. _____ are bonds issued by governments, authorities, or public benefit corporations that are guaranteed by the revenue flow of the issuing agency.

The Supreme Court decision of Pollock versus Farmer's Loan and Trust Company of 1895 initiated a wave or series of innovations for the financial services community in both tax-treatment and regulation from government. This specific case, according to a leading investment bank's research, resulted in the 'intergovernmental tax immunity doctrine,' ultimately leading to 'tax-free status.' Municipal bonds are generally exempt from federal tax on their interest payments (not capital gains.)

a. Callable bond
c. Municipal bond
b. Zero-coupon bond
d. Revenue bonds

22. In finance, _____ is the process of estimating the potential market value of a financial asset or liability. They can be done on assets (for example, investments in marketable securities such as stocks, options, business enterprises, or intangible assets such as patents and trademarks) or on liabilities (e.g., Bonds issued by a company.) A _____ is required in many contexts including investment analysis, capital budgeting, merger and acquisition transactions, financial reporting, taxable events to determine the proper tax liability, and in litigation.

a. Disclosure
c. Daybook
b. Valuation
d. Vyborg Appeal

23. The _____ of a bond is the amount of interest paid per year expressed as a percentage of the face value of the bond. It is the interest rate that a bond issuer will pay to a bondholder.

For example if you hold $10,000 nominal of a bond described as a 4.5% loan stock, you will receive $450 in interest each year (probably in two installments of $225 each.)

a. Callable bond
c. Revenue bonds
b. Convertible bond
d. Coupon rate

24. _____ is the value of a coin, stamp or paper money, as printed on the coin, stamp or bill itself by the minting authority. While the _____ usually refers to the true value of the coin, stamp or bill in question (as with circulation coins) it can sometimes be largely symbolic, as is often the case with bullion coins. For example, a one troy ounce (31 g) American Gold Eagle bullion coin was worth and sold for about $670 USD during 2006 market prices (as of July 17, 2006) and yet has a _____ of only $50 USD.

a. BMC Software, Inc.
b. Face value
c. 3M Company
d. BNSF Railway

25. A _____ is any one of a variety of different systems, institutions, procedures, social relations and infrastructures whereby persons trade, and goods and services are exchanged, forming part of the economy. It is an arrangement that allows buyers and sellers to exchange things. _____s vary in size, range, geographic scale, location, types and variety of human communities, as well as the types of goods and services traded.
   a. Perfect competition
   b. Market Failure
   c. Recession
   d. Market

26. _____ is a life of security. It may also refer to the final payment date of a loan or other financial instrument, at which point all remaining interest and principal is due to be paid.

1, 3, 6 months _____ band can be calculated by using 30-day per month periods. For _____ bands over a year it is acceptable to use 365 day per year. For example with a Treasury Bond, its _____ is the date on which the principal is paid.

   a. Factor
   b. Statements of Financial Accounting Standards No. 133, Accounting for Derivative Instruments and Hedging Activities
   c. The Goodyear Tire ' Rubber Company
   d. Maturity

27. _____, in finance and accounting, means stated value or face value. From this comes the expressions at par (at the _____), over par (over _____) and under par (under _____).

_____ is a nominal value of a security which is determined by an issuer company at a minimum price. _____ of an equity (a stock) is a somewhat archaic concept. The _____ of a stock was the share price upon initial offering; the issuing company promised not to issue further shares below _____, so investors could be confident that no one else was receiving a more favorable issue price. This was far more important in unregulated equity markets than in the regulated markets that exist today.

   a. Creditor
   b. Restructuring
   c. Net worth
   d. Par value

28. In finance, the term _____ describes the amount in cash that returns to the owners of a security. Normally it does not include the price variations, at the difference of the total return. _____ applies to various stated rates of return on stocks (common and preferred, and convertible), fixed income instruments (bonds, notes, bills, strips, zero coupon), and some other investment type insurance products (e.g. annuities.)
   a. Residence trusts
   b. Disclosure
   c. Pension System
   d. Yield

29. A _____ assesses the credit worthiness of an individual, corporation, or even a country. It is an evaluation made by credit bureaus of a borrower's overall credit history. They are calculated from financial history and current assets and liabilities.

a. Credit rating
b. Loan
c. Debt
d. Debenture

30. In economics, a _____ is a lower rated, potentially higher paying bond.

- High-yield debt

A high-risk, non-investment-grade bond with a low credit rating, usually BB or lower; as a consequence, it usually has a high yield. opposite of investment-grade bond. This content can be found on the following page:

a. BMC Software, Inc.
b. BNSF Railway
c. 3M Company
d. Junk bond

31. _____ is the process of increasing, or accounting for, an amount over a period of time. Particular instances of the term include:

- _____, the allocation of a lump sum amount to different time periods, particularly for loans and other forms of finance, including related interest or other finance charges.
    - _____ schedule, a table detailing each periodic payment on a loan (typically a mortgage), as generated by an _____ calculator.
    - Negative _____, an _____ schedule where the loan amount actually increases through not paying the full interest
- Amortized analysis, analyzing the execution cost of algorithms over a sequence of operations.
- _____ of capital expenditures of certain assets under accounting rules, particularly intangible assets, in a manner analogous to depreciation.
- _____

a. Annuity
b. Intangible
c. EBIT
d. Amortization

32. _____ is a fee paid on borrowed assets. It is the price paid for the use of borrowed money , or, money earned by deposited funds .Assets that are sometimes lent with _____ include money, shares, consumer goods through hire purchase, major assets such as aircraft, and even entire factories in finance lease arrangements. The _____ is calculated upon the value of the assets in the same manner as upon money.

a. Insolvency
b. AIG
c. Interest
d. ABC Television Network

33. _____ were published by Accounting Principles Board (APB.) The board was created by American Institute of Certified Public Accountants (AICPA) in 1959 and was replaced by Financial Accounting Standards Board (FASB) in 1973. Its mission was to develop an overall conceptual framework of US generally accepted accounting principles (US GAAP.)

a. Accounting Principles Board Opinions
b. ABC Television Network
c. AMEX
d. AIG

34. In accounting, _____ or carrying value is the value of an asset according to its balance sheet account balance. For assets, the value is based on the original cost of the asset less any depreciation, amortization or impairment costs made against the asset. Traditionally, a company's _____ is its total assets minus intangible assets and liabilities.
- a. Book value
- b. Matching principle
- c. Depreciation
- d. Generally accepted accounting principles

35. _____ is the concept of adding accumulated interest back to the principal, so that interest is earned on interest from that moment on. The act of declaring interest to be principal is called compounding (i.e., interest is compounded.) A loan, for example, may have its interest compounded every month: in this case, a loan with $100 principal and 1% interest per month would have a balance of $101 at the end of the first month.
- a. Kanban
- b. Risk management
- c. Trademark
- d. Compound interest

36. _____ are formal bookkeeping and accounting terms. They are the most fundamental concepts in accounting, representing the two records that one party in a transaction makes on its records, transferring a money balance from one account to another, one representing a reduction of liability or increase in asset, and the other representing a balancing increase in liability or reduction of asset.

Debits and credits are a system of notation used in accounting to keep track of money movements (transactions) into and out of an account.

- a. Bookkeeping
- b. Controlling account
- c. Cookie jar accounting
- d. Debit and credit

37. In economics, business, retail, and accounting, a _____ is the value of money that has been used up to produce something, and hence is not available for use anymore. In economics, a _____ is an alternative that is given up as a result of a decision. In business, the _____ may be one of acquisition, in which case the amount of money expended to acquire it is counted as _____.
- a. Cost
- b. Cost of quality
- c. Prime cost
- d. Cost allocation

38. Treasury securities are government debt issued by the United States Department of the Treasury through the Bureau of the Public Debt. They are the debt financing instruments of the U.S. Federal government, and they are often referred to simply as Treasuries or Treasurys. There are four types of marketable treasury securities: Treasury bills, Treasury notes, _____, and Treasury Inflation Protected Securities (TIPS.)

_____ have the longest maturity, from twenty years to thirty years. They have a coupon payment every six months like T-Notes, and are commonly issued with maturity of thirty years.

- a. BNSF Railway
- b. 3M Company
- c. BMC Software, Inc.
- d. Treasury bonds

Chapter 14. Long-Term Liabilities,

39. The _____ is a private, not-for-profit organization whose primary purpose is to develop generally accepted accounting principles (GAAP) within the United States in the public's interest. The Securities and Exchange Commission (SEC) designated the _____ as the organization responsible for setting accounting standards for public companies in the U.S. It was created in 1973, replacing the Accounting Principles Board and the Committee on Accounting Procedure of the American Institute of Certified Public Accountants. The _____'s mission is 'to establish and improve standards of financial accounting and reporting for the guidance and education of the public, including issuers, auditors, and users of financial information.'

The _____ is not a governmental body.

   a. Fannie Mae
   c. Governmental Accounting Standards Board

   b. Public company
   d. Financial Accounting Standards Board

40. _____ occurs when an entity that has issued callable bonds calls those debt securities from the debt holders with the express purpose of reissuing new debt at a lower coupon rate. In essence, the issue of new, lower-interest debt allows the company to prematurely refund the older, higher-interest debt.

On the contrary, NonRefundable Bonds may be callable but they cannot be re-issued with a lower coupon rate.

   a. Manufacturing operations
   c. Lump sum

   b. Redemption value
   d. Refunding

41. The phrase _____, according to the Organization for Economic Co-operation and Development, refers to 'creative work undertaken on a systematic basis in order to increase the stock of knowledge, including knowledge of man, culture and society, and the use of this stock of knowledge to devise new applications [sic]'

New product design and development is more than often a crucial factor in the survival of a company. In an industry that is fast changing, firms must continually revise their design and range of products. This is necessary due to continuous technology change and development as well as other competitors and the changing preference of customers.

   a. BNSF Railway
   c. 3M Company

   b. BMC Software, Inc.
   d. Research and development

42. _____ in economics and business is the result of an exchange and from that trade we assign a numerical monetary value to a good, service or asset. If Alice trades Bob 4 apples for an orange, the _____ of an orange is 4 apples. Inversely, the _____ of an apple is 1/4 oranges.

   a. Price discrimination
   c. Price

   b. Transactional Net Margin Method
   d. Discounts and allowances

43. A _____, also referred to as a note payable in accounting, is a contract where one party (the maker or issuer) makes an unconditional promise in writing to pay a sum of money to the other (the payee), either at a fixed or determinable future time or on demand of the payee, under specific terms. They differ from IOUs in that they contain a specific promise to pay, rather than simply acknowledging that a debt exists.

The terms of a note typically include the principal amount, the interest rate if any, and the maturity date.

Chapter 14. Long-Term Liabilities,

a. 3M Company
c. BNSF Railway
b. BMC Software, Inc.
d. Promissory note

44. _____ is any physical or virtual entity that is owned by an individual or jointly by a group of individuals. An owner of _____ has the right to consume, sell, rent, mortgage, transfer and exchange his or her _____. Important widely-recognized types of _____ include real _____, personal _____ (other physical possessions), and intellectual _____ (rights over artistic creations, inventions, etc.), although the latter is not always as widely recognized or enforced.

a. Primary authority
c. Disclosure requirement
b. Fiduciary
d. Property

45. An _____ is the price a borrower pays for the use of money they do not own, for instance a small company might borrow from a bank to kick start their business, and the return a lender receives for deferring the use of funds, by lending it to the borrower. _____s are normally expressed as a percentage rate over the period of one year.

_____s targets are also a vital tool of monetary policy and are used to control variables like investment, inflation, and unemployment.

a. AMEX
c. ABC Television Network
b. Interest rate
d. AIG

46. An _____ is a mortgage loan where the interest rate on the note is periodically adjusted based on a variety of indices. Among the most common indices are the rates on 1-year constant-maturity Treasury (CMT) securities, the Cost of Funds Index (COFI), and the London Interbank Offered Rate (LIBOR.) A few lenders use their own cost of funds as an index, rather than using other indices.

a. Adjustable rate mortgage
c. AMEX
b. AIG
d. ABC Television Network

47. A _____ is the transfer of an interest in property (or the equivalent in law - a charge) to a lender as a security for a debt - usually a loan of money. While a _____ in itself is not a debt, it is the lender's security for a debt. It is a transfer of an interest in land (or the equivalent) from the owner to the _____ lender, on the condition that this interest will be returned to the owner when the terms of the _____ have been satisfied or performed.

a. BNSF Railway
c. Mortgage
b. 3M Company
d. BMC Software, Inc.

48. A _____ or floating rate mortgage is a mortgage loan where the interest rate varies to reflect market conditions.

The interest rate will normally vary with changes to the base rate of the central bank and reflects changing costs on the credit markets. This method of variation directly linked to underlying costs benefits lenders by ensuring a profit by passing the interest rate risk to the borrower.

a. Prime rate
c. Reserve requirement
b. Transactional account
d. Variable rate mortgage

Chapter 14. Long-Term Liabilities,

49. A _____ is a contract conferring a right on one person to possess property belonging to another person (called a landlord or lessor) to the exclusion of the owner landlord. It is a rental agreement between landlord and tenant. The relationship between the tenant and the landlord is called a tenancy, and the right to possession by the tenant is sometimes called a leasehold interest.
    a. Robinson-Patman Act
    b. Model Code of Professional Responsibility
    c. Federal Sentencing Guidelines
    d. Lease

50. An _____ is a lease whose term is short compared to the useful life of the asset or piece of equipment (an airliner, a ship etc.) being leased. An _____ is commonly used to acquire equipment on a relatively short-term basis.
    a. Express warranty
    b. Issued shares
    c. Operating lease
    d. Employee Retirement Income Security Act

51. A _____, in business matters, is an entity that is controlled by a bigger and more powerful entity. The controlled entity is called a company, corporation, or limited liability company, and the controlling entity is called its parent (or the parent company.) The reason for this distinction is that a lone company cannot be a _____ of any organization; only an entity representing a legal fiction as a separate entity can be a _____.
    a. 3M Company
    b. Parent company
    c. BMC Software, Inc.
    d. Subsidiary

52. The U.S. _____ is an independent agency of the United States government which holds primary responsibility for enforcing the federal securities laws and regulating the securities industry, the nation's stock and options exchanges, and other electronic securities markets. The SEC was created by section 4 of the Securities Exchange Act of 1934 (now codified as 15 U.S.C. ÂÂ§ 78d and commonly referred to as the 1934 Act.)
    a. BNSF Railway
    b. BMC Software, Inc.
    c. 3M Company
    d. Securities and Exchange Commission

53. A _____ is a fungible, negotiable instrument representing financial value. they are broadly categorized into debt securities (such as banknotes, bonds and debentures), and equity securities; e.g., common stocks. The company or other entity issuing the _____ is called the issuer.
    a. BMC Software, Inc.
    b. Tracking stock
    c. 3M Company
    d. Security

54. In economics, _____ or _____ goods or real _____ refers to factors of production used to create goods or services that are not themselves significantly consumed (though they may depreciate) in the production process. _____ goods may be acquired with money or financial _____. In finance and accounting, _____ generally refers to financial wealth, especially that used to start or maintain a business.
    a. Capital
    b. Vyborg Appeal
    c. Screening
    d. Disclosure

55. In finance, _____ refers to the way a corporation finances its assets through some combination of equity, debt, or hybrid securities. A firm's _____ is then the composition or 'structure' of its liabilities. For example, a firm that sells $20 billion in equity and $80 billion in debt is said to be 20% equity-financed and 80% debt-financed.
    a. Flow-through entity
    b. Capital Structure
    c. Gross income
    d. Restricted stock

56. _____ means the giving out of information, either voluntarily or to be in compliance with legal regulations or workplace rules.

- In Computer security, full _____ means disclosing full information about vulnerabilities.
- In computing, _____ widget
- Journalism, full _____ refers to disclosing the interests of the writer which may bear on the subject being written about, for example, if the writer has worked with an interview subject in the past.

- In law:
    - The law of England and Wales, _____ refers to a process that may form part of legal proceedings, whereby parties inform to other parties the existence of any relevant documents that are, or have been, in their control. This compares with the process known as discovery in the course of legal proceedings in the United States.
    - In U.S. civil procedure (litigation rules for civil cases), _____ is a stage prior to trial. In civil cases, each party must disclose to the opposing party the following: names of witnesses which it may use to support its side, copies of documents (or mere description of these documents) in its control which it may use to support its side, computation of damages claimed, and certain insurance information. _____ is related to, but technically prior to, the discovery stage.
    - In Company law (known as 'corporate law' in the United States), _____ refers to giving out information about public or limited companies or their officers, which might be kept secret if the company was a private company or a partnership.

- In real property transactions, _____ refers to providing to a buyer information known to the seller or broker/agent concerning the condition or other aspects of real property that would affect the property's value or desirability. These rules regarding what information must be disclosed, and whether the information must be disclosed even if a buyer does not ask, vary from one jurisdiction to the next.

a. Tax harmonisation
c. Trailing
b. Controlled Foreign Corporations
d. Disclosure

57. In economics, the concept of the _____ refers to the decision-making time frame of a firm in which at least one factor of production is fixed. Costs which are fixed in the _____ have no impact on a firms decisions. For example a firm can raise output by increasing the amount of labour through overtime.

a. Long-run
c. 3M Company
b. BMC Software, Inc.
d. Short-run

58. _____ or interest coverage ratio is a measure of a company's ability to honor its debt payments. It may be calculated as either EBIT or EBITDA divided by the total interest payable.

a. Times interest earned
c. Return of capital
b. Yield Gap
d. Capital recovery factor

Chapter 14. Long-Term Liabilities,

59. In business and accounting, _____ are everything of value that is owned by a person or company. It is a claim on the property your income of a borrower. The balance sheet of a firm records the monetary value of the _____ owned by the firm.
   a. Earnings before interest, taxes, depreciation and amortization
   b. Accrual basis accounting
   c. Accounts receivable
   d. Assets

60. A _____ is a party (e.g. person, organization, company, or government) that has a claim to the services of a second party. It is a person or institution to whom money is owed. The first party, in general, has provided some property or service to the second party under the assumption (usually enforced by contract) that the second party will return an equivalent property or service.
   a. Treasury company
   b. Payback period
   c. Creditor
   d. Par value

61. A _____ is a type of debt Like all debt instruments, a _____ entails the redistribution of financial assets over time, between the lender and the borrower.
   a. Debenture
   b. Loan to value
   c. Lender
   d. Loan

62. In financial accounting and finance, _____ is the portion of receivables that can no longer be collected, typically from accounts receivable or loans. _____ in accounting is considered an expense.

There are two methods to account for _____:

1. Direct write off method (Non - GAAP)

A receivable which is not considered collectible is charged directly to the income statement.

1. Allowance method (GAAP)

An estimate is made at the end of each fiscal year of the amount of _____. This is then accumulated in a provision which is then used to reduce specific receivable accounts as and when necessary.

   a. 3M Company
   b. Bad debt
   c. Total Expense Ratio
   d. Tax expense

63. In economics a _____ is an entity that owes a debt to someone else. The entity may be an individual, a firm, a government, a company or other legal person. The counterparty is called a creditor.
   a. Fair market value
   b. Debtor
   c. Segregated portfolio company
   d. Shares authorized

64. _____ is the corporate management term for the act of partially dismantling or otherwise reorganizing a company for the purpose of making it more profitable. Also known as corporate _____, debt _____ and financial _____.

_____ is often done as part of a bankruptcy or of a strategic takeover by another firm, such as a leveraged buyout by a private equity firm.

a. Net worth
b. Restructuring
c. Fair market value
d. Payback period

65. The term _____ describes a reduction in recognized value. In accounting terminology, it refers to recognition of the reduced or zero value of an asset. In income tax statements, it refers to a reduction of taxable income as recognition of certain expenses required to produce the income.
   a. Current asset
   b. Salvage value
   c. Payroll
   d. Write-off

66. In accounting, _____ has a very specific meaning. It is an outflow of cash or other valuable assets from a person or company to another person or company. This outflow of cash is generally one side of a trade for products or services that have equal or better current or future value to the buyer than to the seller.
   a. ABC Television Network
   b. AMEX
   c. Expense
   d. AIG

67. In financial accounting, a _____ or statement of financial position is a summary of a person's or organization's balances. Assets, liabilities and ownership equity are listed as of a specific date, such as the end of its financial year. A _____ is often described as a snapshot of a company's financial condition.
   a. Balance sheet
   b. Financial statements
   c. Statement of retained earnings
   d. 3M Company

68. Briggs could refer to:

- Briggs cliff, a fictional place in Fullmetal Alchemist manga
- Briggs (crater), a lunar crater
- Briggs Initiative, either of two pieces of Californian legislation sponsored by John Briggs
- Briggs Islet, Tasmania, Australia
- Briggs, Oklahoma, USA
- Briggs, Texas, USA
- _____, a manufacturer of air-cooled gasoline engines
- The Briggs - a punk rock band
- Myers-Briggs Type Indicator

- Anne Briggs, English folk singer
- Ansel Briggs, American politician
- Arthur E. Briggs, California politician
- Asa Briggs, British historian
- Barbara Briggs, American dramatist
- Barbara G. Briggs, Australian botanist
- Barry Briggs, New Zealand World Motorcycle speedway champion
- Barry Bruce-Briggs, public policy writer
- Benjamin Briggs, captain of the Mary Celeste
- Bill Briggs, American skier
- Billy Briggs, American musician
- Bobby Briggs, fictional character from Twin Peaks
- Charles Augustus Briggs, American theologian
- Charles Frederick Briggs, American journalist
- Clare Briggs, American comics artist
- David Briggs:
    - David Briggs (producer) (1944-1995), American record producer
    - David Briggs (composer) English organist and composer
    - David Briggs (Australian musician), guitarist with Little River Band and Australian record producer
- Derek Briggs, Irish paleontologist
- Everett Francis Briggs, (1908-2006), American Catholic priest
- Frank A. Briggs, American politician
- Frank O. Briggs, American politician
- Frank P. Briggs, American politician
- Gary Briggs (musician), British guitarist
- Gary Briggs (footballer), British footballer
- George N. Briggs, American politician
- Major Garland Briggs, fictional character from Twin Peaks
- Harold Briggs
    - Harold Briggs (General), British general
    - Harold Briggs (politician), British Conservative MP
- Henry Briggs (politician)
- Henry Briggs (mathematician), English mathematician
- Hortense Briggs, fictional character from An American Tragedy by Theodore Dreiser
- Ian Briggs, television writer
- Jack Briggs, American instrument maker
- James Briggs, any of several people
- Jason W. Briggs, American Latter Day Saint leader
- Jeff Briggs, American computer games executive
- Joe Bob Briggs, pseudonym of John Irving Bloom, film critic and actor
- John Briggs (politician), a California politician
- John Briggs (author)
- Johnny Briggs:

- - Johnny Briggs (cricketer)
  - Johnny Briggs (actor), actor who played Mike Baldwin on the British soap opera Coronation Street
  - Johnny Briggs (baseball), a former Major League Baseball outfielder
- Jon Briggs, British radio personality
- Jonny Briggs, BBC children's television programme first broadcast in 1985.
- Karen Briggs, American violinist
- Katharine Cook Briggs, co-inventor of the Myers-Briggs Type Indicator personality test
- Katharine Mary Briggs, British author
- Kevin 'She'kspere' Briggs, American record producer
- Lance Briggs, American football player
- LeBaron Russell Briggs, American educator
- Lyman James Briggs, American physicist and civil servant
- Matilda Briggs, passenger on the Marie Celeste
- Matthew Briggs, English footballer
- Nicholas Briggs, British actor
- Nigel Briggs, Singer/Song writer
- Patricia Briggs, American fantasy writer
- Paul Briggs, Australian boxer
- Raymond Briggs, British illustrator and author
- Sandra Briggs, fictional character from Emmerdale
- Shannon Briggs, American boxer
- Stephen Briggs, British Discworld adapter
- Stephen Foster Briggs, American engineer, co-founder of The _____ Company
- Ted Briggs, British seaman
- Tom Briggs, American football player
- Walter Briggs, Major League Baseball owner

a. Briggs ' Stratton
c. BNSF Railway
b. 3M Company
d. BMC Software, Inc.

69. Procter is a surname, and may also refer to:

- Bryan Waller Procter (pseud. Barry Cornwall), English poet
- Goodwin Procter, American law firm
- _____, consumer products multinational

a. Welfare
c. Markup
b. Screening
d. Procter ' Gamble

Chapter 1

1. d	2. d	3. d	4. b	5. d	6. d	7. b	8. d	9. a	10. d
11. d	12. d	13. b	14. c	15. d	16. a	17. d	18. c	19. d	20. b
21. a	22. d	23. a	24. a	25. d	26. d	27. b	28. c	29. d	30. c
31. c	32. d	33. d	34. d	35. d	36. b	37. c	38. a	39. d	40. d
41. b	42. d	43. d	44. d	45. a	46. d				

Chapter 2

| 1. d | 2. c | 3. a | 4. d | 5. d | 6. d | 7. d | 8. c | 9. d |

Chapter 3

1. a	2. d	3. b	4. a	5. d	6. b	7. b	8. b	9. d	10. d
11. d	12. d	13. d	14. d	15. d	16. c	17. a	18. a	19. b	20. d
21. a	22. d	23. d	24. d	25. d	26. b	27. d	28. c	29. b	30. c
31. d	32. d	33. d	34. d	35. d	36. d	37. c	38. a	39. c	40. a
41. d	42. d	43. d	44. d	45. d	46. a	47. d	48. b	49. b	50. d
51. d	52. d	53. d	54. d	55. a	56. d	57. a			

Chapter 4

1. a	2. d	3. b	4. b	5. d	6. b	7. a	8. c	9. d	10. c
11. b	12. a	13. b	14. a	15. d	16. d	17. c	18. d	19. a	20. d
21. d	22. c	23. b	24. d	25. d	26. d	27. d	28. d	29. d	30. b
31. b	32. d								

Chapter 5

1. d	2. d	3. b	4. b	5. d	6. c	7. a	8. d	9. c	10. d
11. d	12. d	13. b	14. d	15. d	16. c	17. d	18. d	19. c	20. d
21. c	22. b	23. d	24. d	25. c	26. a	27. b	28. b	29. b	30. d
31. b	32. d	33. c	34. d	35. d	36. c	37. d	38. d	39. d	40. d
41. c	42. d	43. d	44. d	45. d	46. d	47. c	48. c	49. d	

Chapter 6

1. d	2. c	3. a	4. d	5. b	6. d	7. b	8. a	9. d	10. d
11. d	12. b	13. b	14. c	15. d	16. c	17. a	18. d	19. c	20. d
21. a	22. a	23. d	24. d	25. c	26. d	27. c	28. d	29. a	30. d
31. d	32. d	33. c	34. c	35. d	36. d				

Chapter 7

1. d	2. a	3. a	4. d	5. b	6. c	7. a	8. b	9. d	10. d
11. b	12. d	13. d	14. d	15. d	16. b	17. d	18. b	19. d	20. d
21. b	22. a	23. b	24. d	25. d	26. d	27. d	28. b	29. d	30. a
31. a	32. d	33. b	34. d	35. b	36. b	37. a	38. d	39. d	40. d
41. a	42. d	43. d	44. d	45. b	46. c	47. d	48. d	49. c	50. d
51. c	52. a	53. b	54. a	55. d	56. d	57. a	58. c	59. c	60. c
61. c	62. c	63. d	64. d						

ANSWER KEY

Chapter 8
1. d	2. a	3. d	4. c	5. c	6. d	7. d	8. d	9. d	10. d
11. c	12. d	13. d	14. c	15. a	16. b	17. d	18. d	19. d	20. d
21. b	22. b	23. b	24. d	25. b	26. d	27. a	28. d	29. d	30. d
31. d	32. b	33. a	34. a	35. d	36. d	37. d	38. d	39. b	40. c
41. d	42. d	43. a	44. a	45. a					

Chapter 9
1. a	2. b	3. d	4. d	5. d	6. b	7. b	8. b	9. c	10. b
11. b	12. c	13. d	14. d	15. a	16. b	17. c	18. a	19. a	20. d
21. d	22. a	23. d	24. a	25. c	26. d	27. d	28. d	29. d	30. c
31. d	32. d	33. d	34. a						

Chapter 10
1. a	2. d	3. d	4. d	5. c	6. c	7. d	8. d	9. d	10. a
11. d	12. d	13. c	14. d	15. d	16. d	17. b	18. d	19. d	20. d
21. a	22. d	23. d	24. d	25. b	26. d	27. d	28. a	29. c	30. c
31. d									

Chapter 11
1. b	2. a	3. a	4. d	5. a	6. c	7. d	8. d	9. c	10. b
11. d	12. b	13. d	14. a	15. d	16. d	17. a	18. d	19. b	20. d
21. d	22. c	23. d	24. a	25. a	26. a	27. d	28. d	29. d	30. b
31. d	32. c	33. d	34. d	35. a	36. d	37. b	38. c	39. c	40. b
41. d	42. d	43. d	44. d						

Chapter 12
1. d	2. c	3. d	4. d	5. d	6. a	7. c	8. d	9. a	10. c
11. d	12. d	13. d	14. d	15. b	16. b				

Chapter 13
1. d	2. d	3. a	4. b	5. d	6. d	7. a	8. b	9. d	10. d
11. b	12. a	13. d	14. d	15. d	16. b	17. d	18. b	19. c	20. c
21. a	22. a	23. a	24. d	25. d	26. a	27. a	28. c	29. a	30. a
31. c	32. d	33. d	34. a	35. d	36. d	37. d	38. b	39. d	40. b
41. d	42. d	43. d	44. d	45. b	46. d	47. d	48. a	49. d	50. d
51. a	52. a	53. d	54. d	55. d					

Chapter 14

1. d	2. d	3. b	4. b	5. d	6. d	7. c	8. d	9. d	10. a
11. d	12. d	13. c	14. d	15. c	16. d	17. b	18. a	19. b	20. b
21. d	22. b	23. d	24. b	25. d	26. d	27. d	28. d	29. a	30. d
31. d	32. c	33. a	34. a	35. d	36. d	37. a	38. d	39. d	40. d
41. d	42. c	43. d	44. d	45. b	46. a	47. c	48. d	49. d	50. c
51. d	52. d	53. d	54. a	55. b	56. d	57. d	58. a	59. d	60. c
61. d	62. b	63. b	64. b	65. d	66. c	67. a	68. a	69. d	

www.ingramcontent.com/pod-product-compliance
Lightning Source LLC
Chambersburg PA
CBHW082043230426
43670CB00016B/2761